THE ESSENTIAL COMPANION TO LIFE IN BIBLE TIMES

Essential Bible Companion Series

Essential Bible Atlas

Essential Bible Companion

Essential Bible Companion to the Psalms

Essential Bible Dictionary

Essential Companion to Life in Bible Times

THE ESSENTIAL COMPANION TO LIFE IN BIBLE TIMES

MOISÉS SILVA

ZONDERVAN®

ZONDERVAN.com/
AUTHORTRACKER
follow your favorite authors

ZONDERVAN

The Essential Companion to Life in Bible Times

Requests for information should be addressed to:

Zondervan, *Grand Rapids, Michigan 49530*

Library of Congress Cataloging-in-Publication Data

Silva, Moisés
The essential companion to life in Bible times / Moisés Silva.
p. cm. — (Essential Bible companion series)
ISBN 978-0-310-28688-2 (softcover)
1. Jews — Social life and customs — To 70 A.D. 2. Jews — Antiquities. 3. Bible. O.T. — Criticism, interpretation, etc. 4. Bible. N.T. — Criticism, interpretation, etc. I. Title.
DS112.S488 2011
220.9'5 — dc22 2010034655

Cover design: Kirk Douponce, DogEaredDesign.com
Art Direction: Tammy Johnson
Cover photography: Steve Gardner/Pixelworks Studio; Erich Lessing/Art Resource, NY; Kim Walton/Walton Images
Interior design: Matthew VanZomeren

Printed in the China

---

11 12 13 14 15 16 17 18 19 /CTC/ 23 22 21 20 19 18 17 16 15 14 13 12 11 10 9 8 7 6 5 4 3 2 1

Contents

5. GOVERNMENT

6. RELIGIOUS LIFE

Preface

The central message of the Bible is clear to any reader. No great education is needed to understand the truths of the gospel and what God requires of us.

Those who wish to "dig deeper," however, find it especially helpful to gain some knowledge of the cultural context in which the Bible was written. Information about its historical setting and about ancient customs can shed wonderful light on the text of Scripture.

Extensive and detailed information of this type can be found in the five-volume *Zondervan Encyclopedia of the Bible* and, more briefly, in the one-volume *Zondervan Illustrated Bible Dictionary*. But because the material in those reference works is organized alphabetically, readers who wish to obtain knowledge of broad subjects need to consult a wide variety of separate articles and to integrate the data into a coherent whole.

The content of the present book is derived from those two works, but the material is reorganized on a topical basis. Moreover, the text has at times been revised and adapted so that it becomes more useful in its new setting.

It is our hope that many Bible students will be encouraged and helped by this new presentation.

Abbreviations

AD	Anno Domini (Year of our Lord)
BC	Before Christ
c.	circa (about, approximately)
cf.	confer (compare)
e.g.	exempli gratia (for example)
et al.	et alii (and others)
ft.	feet
i.e.	id est (that is)
in.	inches
KJV	King James Version
NASB	New American Standard Bible
NIV	New International Version (1984 ed.)
NRSV	New Revised Standard Version
NT	New Testament
OT	Old Testament
TNIV	Today's New International Version

Chapter 1

Family

As the fundamental unit of human society, the family played a central role in Israelite history and culture. This chapter explores the role of individuals in family life from birth until death.

Children

As in other cultures, so also in Israel the birth of a child was a very joyful occasion (Lk. 1:57–58). Moreover, having many children was seen as a special blessing from God:

> Sons are a heritage from the LORD,
> children a reward from him.
> Like arrows in the hands of a warrior
> are sons born in one's youth.
> Blessed is the man
> whose quiver is full of them.
> They will not be put to shame
> when they contend with their
> enemies in the gate. (Ps. 127:3–5)

Conversely, to be a wife without motherhood was regarded not merely as a matter of regret, but also of reproach and humiliation, as may be seen from Rachel's passionate words to her husband Jacob, "Give me children, or I'll die!" (Gen. 30:1), and from Hannah's silent pleading (1 Sam. 1:10–17). It is significant that the wives of the Hebrew patriarchs—Sarah, Rebekah, Rachel (but not Leah)—were by nature barren (Gen. 11:30; 25:21; 29:31), and therefore God's special intervention in their lives showed his favor to Israel (cf. also Elizabeth, Lk. 1:5–25).

According to the Hebrew ceremonial system, childbirth rendered a mother "unclean" because of the bleeding involved (Lev. 12:1–5). After the period of purification was over, she was to bring to the priest a lamb and a pigeon (or dove) to be sacrificed. If she could not afford a lamb, she was allowed to offer a second pigeon instead (12:6–8). The fact that Mary offered two pigeons after the birth of Jesus gives touching testimony to the family's comparative poverty (Lk. 2:22–24).

In the case of a boy, circumcision—the cutting off of his foreskin—was to be performed on the eighth day (Lev. 12:3), at which time the child was officially given his name (Lk. 1:59). Although circumcision was practiced in Egypt and elsewhere, this ritual was especially significant among the Hebrews, for it gave witness to the unique covenant that God had established with Abraham, the father of the nation (Gen. 17:9–14). According to the terms of the covenant, the Lord undertook to be the God of Abraham and his descendants, and they were to belong to him, worshipping and obeying only him. Circumcision reminded the Israelites of God's promises to them and of the duties they had assumed.

The Bible emphasizes that the outward rite, to have any significance, must be accompanied by a "circumcision of the heart" (cf. Lev. 26:41; Deut. 30:6; Ezek.

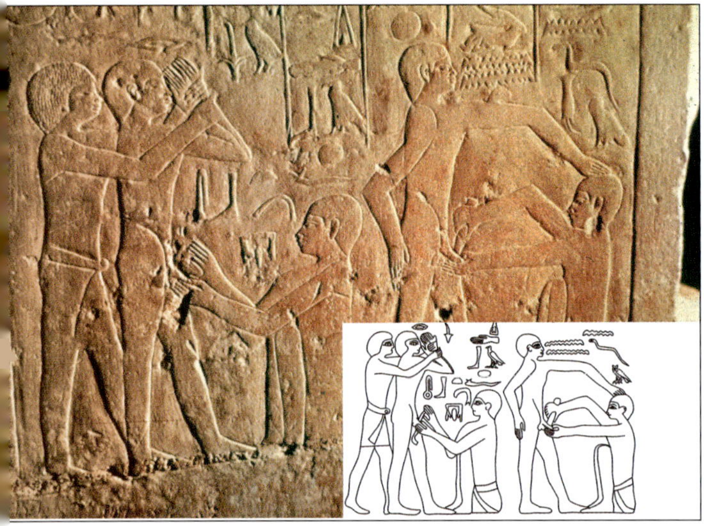

This Egyptian relief depicting circumcision is found in one of the tombs at the Saqqara pyramids (c. 2200 BC).

Z. Radovan/www.BibleLandPictures.com

44:7). Faithless Israelites were no better than the pagans, for they were "uncircumcised in heart" (Jer. 9:25–26; cf. Rom. 2:25–29). In the early history of the Christian church, some Jewish Christians argued for the necessity of circumcising Gentiles who came into the church (Acts 15:1–5). Paul, however, insisted that the signs of the old covenant should not be forced on the children of the new covenant (Gal. 2:3–5; 5:1–6). Paul's view was affirmed by the Council of Jerusalem (Acts 15:22–29).

On the basis of 1 Sam. 1:22–24 and other evidence, most historians believe that mothers in Israel and neighboring countries nursed their babies for approximately three years. Because conception is less likely to occur during the time that a mother is breast-feeding, some have argued that, on average, Israelite women gave birth to four children. Taking into account the high mortality rate of ancient times, we may infer that the typical family was not large, though undoubtedly there would have been many exceptions.

The ancient synagogue in Gamla. The room on the top left may have been where rabbis would teach their students.

© Israel images/Alamy

The education of children in the home was primarily religious (cf. Gen. 18:19). The goal was to train the young to know and serve the Lord (Deut. 6:7; Prov. 1:7) so that throughout their life they would not depart from this way (Prov. 22:6). Thus religious education was concerned with the forming of the child's character. The duty of honoring one's parents was written into the most basic body of laws of the nation, the Ten Commandments (Exod. 20:12). Knowledge was not divorced from being and doing, and good character was seen to result from a right relationship with God through the study of the Torah (God's law or instruction). The Hebrews became known as "the people of the Book." It was this that separated them from all other people.

The Jewish system of education was the result of a long and gradual development from a simple origin to a more complex organization by NT times. Throughout the OT period there was nothing like a state educational system. Generally speaking, the boys were taught the necessary skills of agriculture by their fathers, and the girls were taught domestic skills by their mothers.

It is impossible to say what proportion of the population was taught to read and write, but it is likely that only a small percentage would have been literate. The evidence we have would suggest that prior to and during the monarchy, education of a formal nature was only for the few. Such teaching was done in the homes by the parents. In the exilic and postexilic periods, education expanded its scope to many more individuals and was carried out in Aramaic as well as Hebrew. Such teaching continued to be done in the home, but also in schools and by specialized individuals such as the scribes. With the coming of the Greeks in the fourth century BC, the Greek language too was used in Israelite education.

The Hebrew educational system lacked scientific character. We find nothing of physics, chemistry, biology, psychology, and the other natural sciences. But the Hebrews knew many practical trades and skills: building, mining, metallurgy, wood, and stone work (Exod. 35:30–35). The point of significance is that there were no schools to teach these trades; rather, they were learned in apprenticeships. As far as we know, there were no schools of music, architecture,

This replica of the Siloam inscription shows ancient Hebrew writing.

Wikimedia Commons

sculpture, painting, arts, or the theater. The place that music played in the worship in Israel (see chap. 4) suggests that at least this art must have been developed by systematic instruction, but evidence is lacking. Most of the cultural arts here mentioned were associated with the heathen religions and were developed in Greek and Roman culture.

The development of schools in the more formal sense is related to the growth of the synagogue (see chap. 6). It does not seem likely that a school system was in operation in the time of the exile. During the intertestamental period, literacy must have been widespread, since copies of "the books of the law" were found in many houses (see 1 Macc. 1:56–57). The first elementary school was probably in Jerusalem around NT times, with the institution spreading to the urban centers at a later time, usually under the wing of the synagogue. Joseph ben Gamala (c. AD 65) tried to make elementary education universal and compulsory by endeavoring to provide teachers in all provinces and allowing children to enter the school at the age of six or seven. Instruction was given in reading, and the Torah was studied in both its written and its oral form (i.e., both the Hebrew Bible and the rabbinic traditions).

Elementary education concluded about the age of fifteen, and promising students could then go on to secondary school, known as *Bet ha-Midrash*, "the house of study." Here the rabbis conducted theological discussions. These academies had more sanctity even than the synagogue. Under the leadership of the rabbi, students discussed the interpretation of the Torah and its application. These discussions became the basis of normative Judaism as embodied later in the Talmud. Paul was educated in the academy of the leading teacher of the time, a Pharisee named Gamaliel (Acts 22:3), who was reportedly the grandson of Hillel, considered by many the most influential Jewish rabbi in antiquity.

Men's and Women's Roles

It is a commonplace to say that Israelite society was patriarchal in nature, but this description can be understood in more than one way. The term *patriarch* commonly refers to the oldest male representative of a family or clan (it is especially applied to the founders of the Hebrew nation, Abraham, Isaac, and Jacob). In a technical sense, the word *patriarchy* refers to a social system in which the father functions as the legal authority of the family, so that the wife (or wives) and children play a subordinate role and are dependent on him; in such a system, descent (and thus inheritance) is usually determined on the basis of the male line. Patriarchy has a direct effect on society more generally, with men assuming positions of power in commerce, government, religion, etc.

This general definition certainly gives an accurate picture of the Israelite nation and, indeed, of most societies throughout history. The adjective *patriarchal*, however, has taken on a distinctively negative sense, suggesting unfairness (as men enjoy a disproportionately large share of power), authoritarianism (as men misuse and abuse their authority), and restrictions on women that are damaging both to them and to the community more generally. To what degree such negative elements were present in Israelite society is a question that different people will answer differently, though there is little doubt that the treatment of women in Israel compared favorably with the situation in neighboring nations.

It is often claimed that Hebrew women were regarded as chattel or property, partly because "your neighbor's wife" is included in the list of household components that the Israelite was not supposed to covet (Exod. 20:17). But such an inference may be reading too much into this commandment, and the biblical material as a whole suggests that, generally speaking, women were treated with considerable dignity. In a very oppressive environment, for example, it is unlikely that a wife could have taken the initiative in commercial transactions (see Prov. 31:16, 18).

The fact that a woman, Deborah, could function both as judge and as prophetess (Jdg. 4:4–5) within the large and influential tribe of Ephraim, evidently without creating social disturbance, says a great deal about the people's attitude. The responsibility of "judging" (NRSV) involved not only making legal decisions but also exercising political rule (thus the NIV translates, "Deborah ... was leading Israel at that time"). This task often meant military leadership as well, and Deborah is best known for her role in defeating a Canaanite army under the command of Sisera (4:6–24; note that in this story another woman, Jael, kills Sisera). One must not infer, of course, that Deborah's experience reflected the position of women in general. But it does demonstrate that Israelite society, though male-dominated, did not view women as some kind of inferior race, incapable of exercising communal responsibilities.

A positive view of the relationship between men and women lies at the very foundation of Hebrew thought in the creation account. The initial description in Gen. 1:26–28 identifies "man" as "male and female," thus placing the man and the woman on an equal footing. The detailed account in chap. 2 does make certain distinctions that give Adam a more prominent role: he is created first; he is given the task of caring for the garden; his body is the source for the creation of Eve. Yet at the end of the story the emphasis lies on their unity and harmony: "The man said, 'This is now bone of my bones and flesh of my flesh; she shall be called "woman," for she was taken out of man.' For this reason a man will leave his father and mother and be united to his wife, and they will become one flesh" (2:23–24).

After the fall into sin, however, God said to the woman, "Your desire will be for your husband, and he will rule over you" (Gen. 3:16). The precise significance of those words is disputed. Some argue that the subordination of the wife to the husband was the direct result of the fall. Others believe that at least some form of submission was already part of the created order. In any case, the words make crystal-clear that sin brought disruption into the marriage relationship and, by implication, into society more broadly. It is hardly surprising, therefore, that we should find disturbing elements in the way that men's and women's roles develop in human history, including the history of the Hebrew people.

To a large extent, the activities of Israelite women were confined to the household. If unmarried, a woman lived in her parents' home and was subject to her father (or an older brother). Within that structure she might become the heir of the father's estate, but only if there were no sons; and in that case the inheritance could not be transferred from her tribe when she married (Num. 27:1–11; 36:6–9).

If married, a woman was subject to her husband, but her role in the household was hardly a passive one. The woman from Shunem, for example, exercised initiative and even authority when she provided a room for the prophet Elisha (2 Ki. 4:8–10). If a wife bore children, her responsibilities as a mother became paramount, and she was viewed as the primary caregiver. The biblical text also calls attention to various domestic tasks, such as making bread, sewing, carrying water, tending sheep, hospitality, and generally providing for her husband and family (Gen. 18:6; 24:11–20; 27:9; 29:6; Exod. 2:16; 35:26; 1 Sam. 2:19; 9:11; 2 Sam. 13:8; Prov. 31:10–31; Lk. 10:38–42; Jn. 12:2). By Roman times the status of the wife had improved, particularly at the higher levels of society. In those households where menial tasks were performed by slaves, the Roman matron occupied a position of respect and was able to indulge in her own special way of life.

Sex, Marriage, and Divorce

In the Bible, sexual intercourse is referred to with expressions that allude to the intimate nature of the act, such as "becoming one flesh with" (Gen. 2:24), "knowing" (literal translation in Gen. 4:1, 17, 25; Jdg. 19:25; Matt. 1:25), and "lying with" someone (Gen. 34:7; Num. 31:17, 18; Deut. 22:22). The Scriptures, especially the Song of Solomon, manifest a clear awareness of the emotional and physical closeness involved. It is taken for granted that a husband and a wife should satisfy each other's sexual needs (Prov. 5:18–19; 1 Cor. 7:3–5). Sexual intercourse outside of marriage is explicitly condemned, as are prostitution, homosexuality, incest, rape, and bestiality (Exod. 20:14, 17; 22:16; Lev. 18:6–18, 23; 19:20; 20:15–16; Mk. 7:21; Rom. 1:21–27; 1 Cor. 5:1–2; 6:9–20; Heb. 13:4).

It appears that girls were married very young, some possibly even in their early teens, though the biblical text does not give specific information about this custom. Marriage was often a means of strengthening and promoting the fortunes of the family. The father was responsible for finding a suitable bride for his son, as when Abraham sent his servant to make marriage arrangements for Isaac (Gen. 24). It is usually assumed that the wishes and feelings of the young people did not play a significant role, yet Rebekah was asked to give her consent to marry Isaac (24:57–58). We also read that Saul's daughter, Michal, expressed her love for David, and this led to their marriage (1 Sam. 18:20–21, 27). On some occasions, parental advice was either ignored or not sought (e.g., Esau, Gen. 26:34–35).

In general, marriages were arranged with relatives or with those of the same clan (a practice known as *endogamy*, in contrast to *exogamy*, the latter referring to marriage outside a specific group). One might marry a member of the same tribe or possibly move outside this circle to marry within another

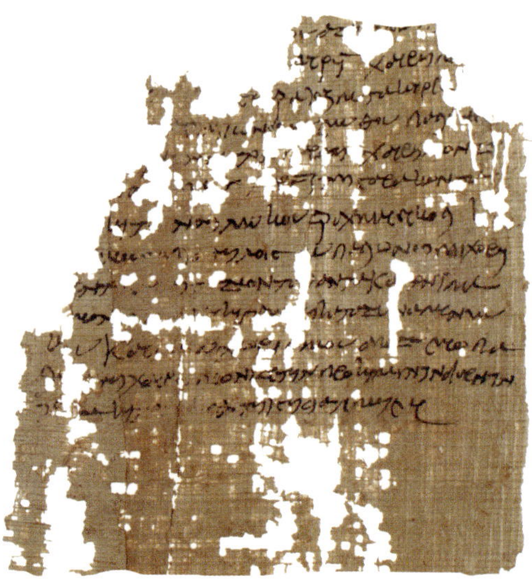

This papyrus, written in Greek, contains an Egyptian marriage contract (AD 143).

Israelite tribe. Marriage to a foreigner was generally discouraged, though some Hebrews took wives from among those women captured in war, while others, such as Samson, received permission from their parents to marry a Philistine woman (Jdg. 14:2–3). Concern was always expressed that marriage with a non-Israelite would dilute the covenantal faith by the introduction of ideas and practices concerning strange gods (1 Ki. 11:4).

Because marriages with close relatives were common, limits of consanguinity are recorded for the Israelites to follow (Lev. 18:6–18). In patriarchal times, a man could marry his half sister on his father's side (Gen. 20:12; cf. 2 Sam. 13:13), but such a union was later forbidden (Lev. 20:17). Cousins, such as Isaac and Rebekah, frequently married. Jacob married two of his cousins, Rachel and Leah, but under the Mosaic law a man was not allowed a simultaneous marriage with two sisters (18:18).

In the ancient world, one important objective of marriage was the maintaining or increasing of family property, and in royal circles many marriages constituted the seal to what in fact were really political alliances. From the time of the patriarchs, wealthy and powerful people were able to indulge in polygamy, but because of the required bride-price, few men could afford more than two wives. One way of circumventing this problem, however, was for a man to have several concubines, and this custom seems to have had quasi-legal sanction in cases where the legitimate wife was barren (e.g., Sarah provided her handmaid Hagar for her husband Abraham, Gen. 16:3). For political reasons, polygamy was popular in royal circles; indeed, Solomon is described as having had "seven hundred wives of royal birth and three hundred concubines" (1 Ki. 11:3). With more than one wife in a household, it was not unusual for strong rivalries to arise (Gen. 29:30–30:2; 1 Sam. 1:5–8).

Despite these examples of polygamy, the most general and acceptable form of marriage was monogamy, as implied by several passages in the law (Exod. 20:17; 21:5; Deut. 5:21; et al.). Jesus pointed to the monogamous relationship between Adam and Eve as the example to be followed (Mk. 10:6–9). In the early church, commitment to one wife was viewed as the proper Christian standard (1 Cor. 7:1–2; 1 Tim. 3:2).

The importance of maintaining and protecting the family name and property led to the institution of *levirate marriage* (from the Latin *lēvir*, "husband's brother"). Where a man died without children, it was the responsibility of the closest male relative, usually his brother, to marry the widow. The first baby born of this union would then be regarded as the child of the dead man and would be entitled to his name and the entire rights of his property. Even if the widow already had children, the male relative would still be expected to marry and support her on the theory that women needed to live under a protector all their lives. Before marriage, a woman was a member of her father's household, and as such she was subject to his authority. At marriage, her husband became her protector, and on his death, through her levirate marriage, she found her new "kinsman redeemer" (Deut. 25:5–10; Ruth 4:1–12).

In addition to finding a bride who was healthy and suitable for the family alliance, parents also had to be aware of the bride price, which may have been viewed either as a gift to the girl's father or as a payment for the loss of her services to her own parents. The amount payable varied according to the "value" of the bride and the social position of the family (1 Sam. 18:23–25). Where it was thought desirable, jewelry, animals, goods, or service could be substituted for gold or silver (Gen. 34:12; 1 Sam. 18:25).

The betrothal (Deut. 28:30; 2 Sam. 3:14) had a particular legal status attached to it that made it almost identical to marriage. The law required that a man committing adultery with a betrothed virgin should be stoned for violating his neighbor's wife (Deut. 22:23–24). A one-year betrothal was considered normal, and it constituted a part of the permanent marriage relationship (Matt. 1:18; Lk. 1:27; 2:5). For one year after being married the groom was exempt from military service (Deut. 24:5) so that the marriage might be established on a proper footing. The bride's father already used the term "son-in-law" from the time of the betrothal (Gen. 19:14), a custom that enhanced the concept of family solidarity.

There remained a distinction between betrothal and marriage, however, especially in the later periods of Jewish history; and although Mary and Joseph were betrothed, and in all other respects she was considered his wife, intercourse would not have taken place until after the marriage, and in this particular situation not until after the birth of Jesus. Following common practice in various cultures, sexual relations possibly were not resumed until after the baby was weaned, at approximately three years of age.

The *wedding ceremony* itself was usually brief, but from early days it became surrounded by an elaborate tradition of ceremony and feasting that was very much in vogue in the time of Christ. Both bride and groom were attired in the finest colorful clothing, the bride being especially resplendent in an elaborate dress. She had previously been washed, perfumed, and decked out with the gold and jewels of her family, together with any personal gifts that she had received.

Toward sunset of the marriage day the groom would set out in procession with his friends, attendants, and musicians for the home of the bride's parents, where she would be waiting with her procession of friends and handmaidens. Then the marriage procession, with the attendant torchbearers, would pass through the village or town streets, to the accompaniment of shouts and singing. At the house where the groom's family lived, the feasting, dancing, and entertainment would normally last for seven days, or occasionally for fourteen (Gen. 29:27; Jdg. 14:12; Tob. 8:20). The crowning of the bride and groom as king and queen of the nuptials dates from the Solomonic period and, with other accretions, became part of the wedding tradition.

In Israel, the option of divorce was available to the husband (Deut. 24:1–4), but it is not clear whether the wife could take the initiative. After the return from exile, wholesale divorce was required of those Israelites who had married foreign wives (Ezra 10). This provision was to ensure that the purity of the Hebrew religion would not be tainted by the influence of those who had grown up with the tradition of strange gods and idolatrous practices.

Normally, however, there was a distinct tendency in Jewish tradition to discourage divorce (Mal. 2:16). When Jesus was questioned about this issue, he stated clearly that divorce does not conform to the divine ideal (Mk. 10:2–12), and Paul also exhorted believers not to divorce their spouses (1 Cor. 7:10–13). Students of the Bible differ among themselves as to which situations, if any, constitute valid exceptions to these instructions.

Old Age and Death

Attainment to old age is frequently recognized in the Bible as a divine blessing, a reward for godliness, and an indication of the favor of God to those who are faithful to his commandments (Job 5:26). Abraham is promised a "good old age" (Gen. 15:15), and long life is pledged to those who respect the authorities established by God (Exod. 20:12).

It is also true, however, that old age brings trials and disabilities. The book of Ecclesiastes graphically describes these problems. Life becomes a burden (Eccl. 12:1); vision is dimmed (v. 2); strength and vigor decline; the teeth disintegrate (v. 3, a calamity before the day of artificial dentures); insomnia develops (v. 4); fears accumulate (v. 5); and desire and ambition wane (v. 5). In the face of these disabilities, however, there is the assurance of God's tender concern (Isa. 46:4) and the anticipation of the hope of glory (Ps. 73:24). It is quite significant that the Lord is depicted not only as a child and as a man in the full strength of his powers, but also as one crowned with white hair (Rev. 1:14), as if to remind human beings that he has relevance for all of life.

In keeping with oriental custom generally, old age is to be respected and honored. Deference to the aged is an expression of the fear of the Lord (Lev. 19:32). Gray hair is to be deemed a mark of honor, not a token of debility (Prov. 20:29). The warning is issued that failure to honor the elderly will surely bring evil upon the nation (Isa. 3:5; Lam. 5:12). It is not that old age, as such, warrants honor and reverence. It must be coupled with integrity and a godly life: "Gray hair is a crown of splendor; / it is attained by a righteous life" (Prov. 16:31). Aged men and women in the church are exhorted to lead lives worthy of respect (Tit. 2:2–5).

It is generally assumed that experience is a valuable teacher and that age brings along with it wisdom and discernment (Job 12:20; 15:10; 32:7). The elderly are regarded as depositaries of knowledge (15:10) and custodians of the tradition. Moses, in his farewell, urged Israel to consult with the fathers and elders (Deut. 32:7). Rehoboam made a fatal error when he spurned the counsel of the elderly (1 Ki. 12:6–16). Positions of leadership and responsibility were usually entrusted to men of age and experience (on the role of elders, see chap. 5).

Whether or not one reaches old age, life must come to an end. The very first reference to death in the OT (Gen. 2:17) gives the basic biblical perspective: death is the result of sin (cf. 3:19; Rom. 5:12). In many places the OT writers expressed their personal feelings, speaking of death (especially early death) as something to be feared and avoided at all costs (e.g., Ps. 6:1–5; 88:1–14; Isa. 38). It was felt that death would cut one off from enjoyment of the covenant blessings, which in the OT were given in terms of the land, the temple, the people, and length of days. If length of days is promised for obedience (Exod. 20:12) and is a sign of God's favor (Job 5:26), then the cutting off of those days, even when long, is an indication that death is something unnatural.

On the other hand, God can take people to himself without their dying (Gen. 5:24;

Ossuary.

Doug Bookman/www.BiblePlaces.com

Funeral procession of Ani, an influential royal scribe in ancient Egypt (c. 1200 BC).

2 Ki. 2:11) and can even restore the dead to life (1 Ki. 17:22; 2 Ki. 4:34; 13:21; Lk. 7:11–16; Jn. 11:38–44). He can completely triumph over death (Isa. 25:8; 26:19; Ezek. 37:11–12; Dan. 12:2; Hos. 13:14; 1 Cor. 15:54–57). Therefore, even in the OT God's people can express confidence in personal resurrection (e.g., Job 19:25–27; Pss. 16:9–11; 17:15; 73:23–26). This hope finds its full flowering in the NT, which reveals Christ as the one "who has destroyed death and has brought life and immortality to light through the gospel" (2 Tim. 1:10).

Among the Jews, as well as people of the ancient Near East generally, burial usually took place within twenty-four hours (cf. Deut. 21:23). Problems of sanitation and fear of possible defilement through contact with a dead body (Num. 9:10–14) constituted reasons for such swiftness. Sometimes very little was done to the body, as shown by Absalom's hasty burial (2 Sam. 18:17). Often the corpse was washed (Acts 9:37) or anointed with aromatic preparations (Mk. 16:1; Jn. 19:39), which was an old practice (2 Chr. 16:14). The body was also wrapped in some cloth or garment (Acts 5:6) or bound up with grave bandages, usually of linen (Mk. 15:46; Jn. 19:40), and the face was evidently covered or bound separately with a face cloth (Jn. 11:44).

The Jews were averse to cremating the corpse, but in some exceptional cases the bodies were indeed burned (Lev. 20:14; 21:9; Josh. 7:15, 25). There is no biblical evidence that embalming, a process so prevalent among the Egyptians, was practiced by the Jews, except in the isolated cases of Jacob and Joseph (Gen. 50:2, 26), since the latter's official position in Egypt dictated the procedure.

Before burial, the body was placed on a bier (literally, "couch, bed," cf. 2 Sam. 3:31; 2 Chr. 16:14 [here possibly a crypt]; Lk. 7:14). Archaeology has shown that pottery storage jars sometimes were used to hold the remains of adults and of infants and small children. Although the Egyptians customarily used the coffin, often elaborately decorated, this object does not seem to have been common among the Jews; it is mentioned in the Bible only in Joseph's case (Gen. 50:26). Some terra-cotta coffins have been discovered in Palestine, and in Hellenistic and Roman times elaborately decorated marble sarcophagi were used.

Although not mentioned in Scripture, ossuaries (bone-boxes) were used early and were quite common in the early Roman period. Rectangular limestone boxes, twenty to thirty inches in length, with personal names and decorations often inscribed on them, have been found near Jerusalem in caves and tombs. These were used for bones after the flesh had decomposed because grave space was needed for other corpses.

Types of burying places included simple holes or pits (sometimes lined with stones or bricks), stone slab dolmen graves (c. 4500 BC), and natural caves and tombs hewn out of rocky hillsides. In the Hellenistic and Roman periods the poor continued to use caves and cisterns, but other hewn tombs became larger and more elaborate. At times tombs included multiple units used by

Collection of ossuaries found at the Dominus Flevit church in Jerusalem.

www.HolyLandPhotos.org

Herod's family tomb. Note the rolling stone.

www.HolyLandPhotos.org

families, as exemplified by Abraham's family tomb at the cave of Machpelah (Gen. 23). Archaeology has shown that often grave areas were reused, parts of old skeletons being pushed aside to make room for the new. Sometimes graves were located beneath the floors of houses; perhaps this practice is alluded to in connection with Samuel's burial (1 Sam. 25:1). Burial grounds for common people were located in the Kidron Valley at Jerusalem (Jer. 26:23; 2 Ki. 23:6).

Mourning for the dead was an essential part of the burial ceremony; it involved great wailing and a shrill cry (Jer. 4:8; 49:3; Joel 1:13; Acts 8:2). The family (Gen. 23:2; 2 Sam. 11:26), friends, and others affected by the death (1 Sam. 25:1; 2 Sam. 1:11–12; Jer. 22:18) participated in it, and tears were shed ritually at the appropriate time (Jer. 9:17–18; Mal. 2:13; Lk. 7:32). The mourning with flute playing took place right after death (Gen. 23:2), at the home where the corpse was resting (Matt. 9:23), and continued on to the tomb (Lk. 7:12–13). The period of mourning lasted ordinarily for seven days (Gen. 50:10; 1 Chr. 10:12; cf. Jdg. 16:24 and Sir. 22:12); for important persons, such as Moses and Aaron, thirty days (Num. 20:29; Deut. 34:8); and, in one case, Jacob, seventy days (Gen. 50:3), according to Egyptian custom. Professional mourners were also important in the death ritual (cf. 2 Chr. 35:25; Jer. 9:17).

Burial was considered a necessary act, the deprival of which, with the resultant exposure to the ravages of beasts, being considered a serious indignity and calamity (2 Ki. 9:36–37; Ezek. 29:5). Even criminals were allowed to be buried (Deut. 21:22–23). The law instructed that touching a corpse brought ceremonial defilement (Lev. 21:1; Num. 19:11–13), but it was considered a proper act to protect the bodies of slain warriors until they could be buried (2 Sam. 21:1–14) and to bury those slain in times of persecution (Tob. 1:17–19; 2:8).

Chapter 2

Household

The previous chapter examined the roles of individuals in family life. Here we look at the context in which families lived: their houses and belongings, their physical sustenance, and their health.

Houses and Furniture

© Zondervan. Artist: Jessica Bowling; Reconstruction/Archaeologist: Daniel Warner

Elaborate houses in the Mesopotamian city of Ur, belonging to the period when Abraham lived there (Gen. 11:31), have been excavated. He abandoned these luxurious surroundings to live in a tent (12:8) in the Land of Promise. The other patriarchs probably lived in tents as well. After the conquest under Joshua, the Israelites came increasingly to live in houses in the cities and towns of Canaan. House walls were often of rough stone as much as 3 ft. thick and often of unburned clay brick (Job 4:19), sometimes protected with a casing of stone slabs. In larger buildings the stones were squared, smoothed, and pointed.

To enter the ordinary small house, from the street one first entered a forecourt, with a covered portion on one side. From the forecourt, doors opened into a living room, with two small bedchambers beyond. When sons married, additions were made as space permitted by using the court, complicating the design. Especially on a hilly site, a large boulder would be built into the corner to support the walls, the most necessary stone being called the cornerstone (Isa. 28:16). The importance of dedicating a new house (in earliest times by sacrifices) was recognized by excusing a man from military duty until he had done so (Deut. 20:5).

Remains of a four-room house in Hazor.

© Kim Walton

Reconstruction of a building in Galilee from the Talmudic period, showing the construction techniques of that period.

www.HolyLandPhotos.org

Korazin basalt roof beams.

Todd Bolen/www.BiblePlaces.com

The floor of a house might be a leveled surface of stone, more often beaten clay; in some cases it was given a thin lime plaster coating. The rich often had a stone slab floor. Solomon's temple had a floor of cypress boards (1 Ki. 6:15). Second floors, supported with stone pillars, were framed and formed as for roofs, with the addition in some cases of the lime plaster topping. Hearths were provided, but no chimney, the smoke escaping through doors and windows. Most baking, however, was done in an outdoor oven.

For doors there were square openings in the wall with a stone or wood lintel, doorposts (Exod. 12:22–23; 1 Ki. 6:31), and a stone threshold. Doors might be of textiles, leather, or rushes, but wooden doors fastened by a bar were used early. Stone sill and head-sockets indicate pivot hinges, requiring sturdier construction of the door. A key is referred to as early as Jdg. 3:25; probably wooden, it may have been a so-called "Egyptian lock," a stick with pins at the end that matched movable pins inside the door (cf. also Cant. 5:4–5).

Windows were high, small openings with covers like the doors for protection; some had lattices. Those in walls fronting inner courts were of larger size. In the house of Rahab, a window looked out over the city wall, a convenient place to observe an attacker as well as to escape, hence the query addressed to her about the spies (cf. Josh. 2:15). At Damascus, the window was high enough above ground to dispense with the lattice, allowing Paul to be lowered to the ground (2 Cor. 11:33).

Roofs had beams with transverse rafters covered with brushwood and overlaid with mud mixed with chopped straw. They were flat and were beaten and rolled. The roof, enclosed by a low wall for safety (Deut. 22:8), could serve as a living area, and even as a bedroom, especially in hot weather (1 Sam. 9:25). It was sometimes used for worship (2 Ki. 23:12; Jer. 19:13; 32:29; Acts 10:9). Three thousand Philistines used the roof of their temple as a grandstand (Jdg. 16:27), illustrating its strength, while its weakness was demonstrated when Samson pushed apart the middle pillars on which the structure depended. There were outside stairs leading to the roof of a house and its "upper chamber." In some cases the "upper room" may have been inside the house.

In the living room a raised brick platform ran across one side of the room (in the Hellenistic period at least), sometimes with ducts to heat it, and on this the family spread their bedding by night or sat by day. In cold weather the cattle might be admitted to the lower part of the living room of a poor family. There was a sharp contrast between the humble homes of the common people and the luxurious dwellings of the very rich in most of the ancient Near East, as well as in Greece and Rome of the Hellenistic period.

A Christian community, many of whose members were slaves, would be familiar with the lavish contents of large houses (2 Tim. 2:20). While Christians at first continued to worship in temple and synagogue, from the beginning they met also in private homes (Acts 1:13; 2:2, 46). Worship in homes was a well-established pattern in Paul's ministry (Rom. 16:5; 1 Cor. 16:19; Col. 4:15; Phlm. 2). Special buildings for Christian churches do not appear in the NT. The family had been the religious unit from the beginning of creation, and worship centered in the house.

Household furniture in biblical Palestine was very simple, varying with the economic status of the householder. Hand-woven curtains separated the men's and the women's quarters. Since houses were primarily a place for sleeping, and people spent most of their

Reconstruction of the upper room in a typical Jewish home in biblical times

Todd Bolen/www.BiblePlaces.com

Guests partaking of a meal in the upper-room guest chamber of a house.

Library of Congress, LC-matpc-02644/www.LifeintheHolyLand.com

A millstone for grinding grain. Erich Lessing/Art Resource, NY

time out of doors, there was little furniture in the house. Mats spread on the bare floor served in place of tables and chairs, though sometimes stone or wooden benches, covered with carpet, were placed along the walls. Chests of various sizes, some highly decorated, provided closed storage for some household items.

Beds were found only in the homes of the wealthy; the average person used sleeping mats, which were rolled up when not in use. With the wealthy it was different, as evident in Amos's denunciation of the nobles of Samaria who, he said, luxuriated in beds of ivory and lazily stretched themselves upon couches (Amos 3:12; 6:4).

If storage room was provided in the house, large storage jars with lids were sunk in the floor for storing oil, grain, and wine. Other rooms stored rough goods, that is, field produce. Where occasion demanded, rooms provided for crafts (e.g., weaving), as shown in tomb models from Egypt.

Lighting for the house was a clay dish with a wick, set either in a pinched rim or in its own spout, the latter being the lamp of Matt. 25:1. Fuel was olive oil. Torches

"Let grain abound throughout the land" (Ps. 72:16).

www.HolyLandPhotos.org

were secured by the use of pitch on a stick. Heating for houses varied according to the climate. Egypt required little, furnished by simple means. In Mesopotamia, braziers were used for both cooking and heating in winter.

Decoration varied from mere whitewashed walls to painted plaster in the better houses, often a painted wainscot, dark in color with a top stripe. Ceilings in some cases were finished with plaster or painted lath. In wealthy homes in Egypt, gold and electrum were used on a stucco base as a lining on low relief. In Mesopotamia, elaborately painted plaster was frequent. Door frames at times were painted red, and in other cases stone slabs as wainscoting provided the only decorative elements.

Men reaping in the fields.
Library of Congress, LC-matpc-02613/www.LifeintheHolyLand.com

Types of Food

The fields of Palestine produced wheat (Gen. 30:14; Ezek. 4:9; et al.), barley (Ruth 1:22; 2:23), millet (Ezek. 4:9), and spelt (Exod. 9:32; Isa. 28:25; Ezek. 4:9). Grain might be shelled out as one went through the fields (Deut. 23:25; Matt. 12:1). When harvested, it was ground into flour to make bread, the main staple in the ancient Near East. Indeed, the word *bread* is often a synonym for food in general. Both wheat bread and barley bread were used. In numerous cases barley bread (Jdg. 7:13; 2 Ki. 4:42) or barley cakes (Ezek. 4:12) are encountered. It was from five barley loaves that Jesus fed the five thousand (Jn. 6:9, 13). Millet and spelt also could be used for bread (Ezek. 4:9). Grain might be parched and eaten (Lev. 23:14; Josh. 5:11; Ruth 2:14; 1 Sam. 17:17; 25:18; 2 Sam. 17:28).

Various kinds of nuts and vegetables are mentioned in the Bible, including pistachio nuts and almonds (Gen. 43:11), beans and lentils (2 Sam. 17:28), and cucumbers (Isa. 1:8; Jer. 10:5). There were the bitter herbs

Almond tree.

Olive press.

www.HolyLandPhotos.org

consumed at Passover (Exod. 12:8; Num. 9:11). A dinner of herbs might suffice for the poor (Prov. 15:17; Rom. 14:2). In times of want the carob pod, ordinarily used for cattle, might be eaten. There was also sweet calamus from a distant land (Jer. 6:20).

The grape produced wine and vinegar (Ruth 2:14) as well as raisins (Num. 6:3; 1 Sam. 25:18; 1 Chr. 12:40; Hos. 3:1). Fresh grapes might be eaten while passing through a vineyard (Deut. 23:24). The spies brought a large cluster of grapes borne on a pole between two of them (Num. 13:23). Raisin cakes were eaten frequently (1 Sam. 25:18; 30:12; 2 Sam. 16:1); they were also used in Canaanite worship (Hos. 3:1).

The fig was eaten fresh (Jer. 24:1–2) and dried (1 Sam. 25:18; 30:12; 1 Chr. 12:40). The first fig of the season was a special delicacy (Isa. 28:4; Jer. 24:2; Hos. 9:10; Mic. 7:1; Nah. 3:12). Sitting under one's own vine and fig tree was considered the ideal state (Mic. 4:4). Dried figs were used for boils (2 Ki. 20:7; Isa. 38:21) and also eaten on journeys (1 Chr. 12:40).

The olive was perhaps eaten both green and ripe as today, though this is not specifically stated. Olives were beaten into oil (Exod. 27:20). The pomegranate (Exod. 28:33; Num. 13:23; 1 Ki. 7:20; Cant. 6:11; 8:2; Joel 1:12) and the apple (Prov. 25:11; Cant. 2:5; 7:8; 8:5; Joel 1:12) were available. The palm tree (Jdg. 4:5; Ps. 92:12; Joel 1:12; Jn. 12:13) and the sycamore (Amos 7:14) are mentioned in Scripture, but no reference is made to their fruit as food. Summer fruits of unspecified variety are often mentioned (Jer. 40:10–12; Amos 8:1).

The domesticated animals supplied meat. The mother and offspring were not to be slaughtered on the same day (Lev. 22:28). The kid of the sheep (2 Sam. 12:3) or goat was a preferred dish (Gen. 31:38; 37:31;

Lev. 4:23, 28; Lk. 15:29). The stalled ox (Prov. 15:17; cf. Amos 6:4; Hab. 3:17) or the fatted calf was reserved for slaughtering on special occasions (1 Sam. 28:24; Matt. 22:4). For such a celebration over the return of the prodigal, the elder brother objected (Lk. 15:30). After the exile there was a Sheep Gate in Jerusalem doubtless so named because the sheep market was near (Neh. 3:1).

A variety of wild game existed to be hunted (cf. Gen. 27:3). Deuteronomy lists seven varieties (Deut. 14:5; cf. Lev. 17:13). There was the wild goat, the ibex, the mountain sheep (Deut. 14:5), the roebuck, the gazelle, the hart (Deut. 12:15), and the antelope (Deut. 14:5; Isa. 51:20).

Fish could be found in the Mediterranean Sea and in the Sea of Galilee (Neh. 13:16; Eccl. 9:12; Jer. 16:16; Ezek. 47:10; Matt. 4:18; Lk. 11:12); in postexilic times fish were sold in the Fish Gate (Neh. 3:3). No specific species are mentioned except good and bad (Matt. 13:48) or big and small (Jon. 1:17; Mk. 8:7; Jn. 21:11). Dried fish were available (Neh. 13:16). Peter, Andrew, James, and John were fishermen prior to their being called to discipleship (Matt. 4:18, 21). The five thousand were fed fish (Matt. 15:34; Mk. 6:38).

From the insect family four types of locusts were eaten (Lev. 11:22–23; cf. Matt. 3:4). Various fowl also provided food (1 Ki. 4:23), including the partridge (1 Sam. 26:20; Jer. 17:11), the quail (Exod. 16:13; Num. 11:32), the pigeon (Lev. 12:6, et al.), the turtledove (Gen. 15:9), and the sparrow (Matt. 10:29; Lk. 12:6). After the Persian period, chickens became available (female, Matt. 23:37; male, 26:34).

Milk from cows, goats, and sheep was used by the Israelites (Deut. 32:14; Prov. 27:27) and kept in skins (Jdg. 4:19). Use of camel milk also may be inferred (cf. Gen. 32:15). Curds (Gen. 18:8, et al.) and cheese (1 Sam. 17:18, et al.), as well as eggs (Deut. 22:6–7; Lk. 11:12; et al.), were also eaten. It should be noted also that honey, both wild and domestic, was known (Gen. 43:11; 1 Sam. 14:25–26; Matt. 3:4; et al.), though it was forbidden in offerings to God (Lev. 2:11).

Food was seasoned with salt (Ezra 6:9; 7:22; Job 6:6), which was obtained by evaporation; the Dead Sea furnished an inexhaustible supply (Ezek. 47:11). Not always pure, there was the possibility of its becoming mixed with foreign matter until it lost its power (Matt. 5:13). Use of pepper is not mentioned in Scripture, but the condiments mint, dill, and cumin (or cummin, Matt. 23:23), coriander seeds (Exod. 16:31; Num. 11:7), and mustard (Matt. 13:31; 17:20; Lk. 13:19; 17:6) made food more palatable.

Olive tree.

Figurine of a woman working a grain mill (Giza, c. 2477 BC).
© Kim Walton, courtesy of the Oriental Institute Museum

One is not to suppose that all this abundance was available at all times and places. Patriarchal fare was doubtless scant. For guests there was bread freshly baked, curds, milk, and the slaughtered young calf (Gen. 18:6, 8). Jacob, on the other hand, dined on bread and pottage of lentils, and for this Esau sold his birthright (25:34); at other times there might be other pottage to make a meal (2 Ki. 4:38). Roasted grain and wine (Ruth 2:14) or bread and wine (Gen. 14:18) might make up the meal of the ordinary person. Victory in battle occasioned feasting from the supplies of the vanquished.

Reconstruction of an ancient kitchen, with a clay-built oven.
Z. Radovan/www.BibleLandPictures.com

Settled life in Palestine brought a greater variety of foods. Abigail brought to David and his men two hundred loaves, two skins of wine, five sheep ready dressed, five measures of parched grain, a hundred clusters of raisins, and two hundred cakes of figs (1 Sam. 25:18; cf. also 2 Sam. 16:1; 17:28–29). Solomon's daily supplies included fine flour, meal, oxen, pasture-fed cattle, sheep, harts, gazelles, roebucks, and fatted fowl (1 Ki. 4:22–23). Tables of the rich were more luxurious than those of nomads and included "choice lambs and fattened calves" (Amos 6:4). An army on the march might have bread, a cake of figs, and clusters of raisins (1 Sam. 30:12). Jesse sent to his sons parched grain and bread, and cheeses to the commander (1 Sam. 17:17–18). Foreign trade added to the variety of foods. Tyre, for example, trafficked in wheat, olives, early figs, honey, oil, and balm (Ezek. 27:17).

Food Preparation

Though royal houses may have had male bakers (Gen. 40:16) and both male and female cooks (1 Sam. 8:13), and though some lesser figures like Samuel had cooks (9:23), the division of labor with the Israelites made food preparation the woman's work (Gen. 18:6; 1 Sam. 8:13; Prov. 31:15). We read, for example, that Tamar took dough, kneaded cakes, baked them, and served them to Ammon (2 Sam. 13:8).

Flour must be ground daily, and the cessation of the sound of the grinding of the mill is the end of a civilization (Eccl. 12:4; Jer. 25:10; Matt. 24:41; Rev. 18:22). Dough consisting of flour and water was kneaded in kneading troughs and baked in an oven to make bread. When baked in haste, it was unleavened bread (Gen. 19:3; Deut. 16:3), but it was more commonly baked with leaven, which was formed from a bit of sour dough left from a previous baking. Bread was sometimes baked on coals (1 Ki. 19:6). In Jerusalem the bakers had a special street in Jeremiah's day (Jer. 37:21).

Meat was boiled in pots (1 Sam. 2:13; Ezek. 24:3–5) or roasted (1 Sam. 2:15; Prov. 12:27); the roasted lamb at Passover was eaten with unleavened bread and bitter herbs (Exod. 12:8, 9). Various types of pots or caldrons were used in boiling. Water was first boiled and the meat added (Ezek. 24:3–5) with salt. The broth left over also was eaten (Jdg. 6:19; Isa. 65:4). Fish were broiled on coals (Lk. 24:42; Jn. 21:9).

Early Israelites probably sat on the ground while they ate, but the host might stand by to serve (Gen. 18:8). Isaac sat when he ate (27:19), as did Jacob's sons (37:25), the Levite and his concubine (Jdg. 19:6), Saul (1 Sam. 20:5, 24), and Samuel (1 Sam. 9:22). Those fed by the miracle of the Lord sat on the ground (Jn. 6:10).

Tables were used quite early. Adoni-Bezek had seventy captive kings at his table (Jdg. 1:7; cf. Ps. 23:5). We read about crumbs falling to a dog under the table (Matt. 15:27; Mk. 7:28). Jesus sat at a table when Mary anointed him (Jn. 12:2). The guests at Esther's banquet, however, reclined on couches (Esth. 7:8). Reclining on the left elbow was a normal posture in NT times (Jn. 13:23). It is likely that the guests dipped food from the common dish. The Pharisees were strict in demanding, for ritual reasons, the prior washing of hands (Mk. 7:3). A blessing said over food was also an established custom in the first century.

Bedouins in Beersheba eating from a tray.
Library of Congress, LC-matpc-02959/www.LifeintheHolyLand.com

Ancient pitchers found in Turkey.
Courtesy of the Oriental Institute of the University of Chicago

Known as a rhyton, this bronze drinking vessel, part of which is shaped like the head of an ibex, comes from ancient Persia.

Marie-Lan Nguyen/Wikimedia Commons

The OT has no reference to a meal earlier than noon; however, too much should not be made of the silence. The disciples of Jesus ate an early morning meal on the seashore after a night of toil (Jn. 21:12). The main meals were at noon and in the evening. The custom of two meals probably goes back to Scripture: "At twilight you will eat meat, and in the morning you will be filled with bread" (Exod. 16:12). The ravens brought Elijah food in the morning and evening (1 Ki. 17:6). In Egypt there was a midday meal (Gen. 43:16), as there was among laborers in Palestine (Ruth 2:14). Supper came after the work was done (Ruth 3:7; Jdg. 19:16–21).

Prohibited Foods

Under the Mosaic law, food regulations dealt with meat and not with vegetable products. The eating of blood was prohibited as early as the days of Noah (Gen. 9:4; cf. Lev. 19:26; 1 Sam. 14:34; Acts 15:20, 29). Flesh of an animal found dead (Lev. 7:24; Deut. 14:21), flesh of an animal torn by beasts (Exod. 22:31; Lev. 7:24; 22:8), and a limb torn from a living animal were forbidden foods. The eating of fat (Lev. 3:16–17; 7:23) and the fat tail (Exod. 29:22; Lev. 3:9) was prohibited and carried the death penalty when this food was a part of a sacrifice (7:25). These parts belonged to the Lord (Gen. 4:4; 1 Sam. 2:16; 2 Chr. 7:7).

Sandstone measuring cups from the Herodian Period found in Jerusalem.

Z. Radovan/www.BibleLandPictures.com

Laws regarding clean and unclean animals, already in part alluded to in the days of the patriarchs (Gen. 7:2–3), are the most significant regulations of the law in matters of food. The prohibitions appear to be primarily ceremonial in nature, and it is uncertain to what extent, if any, they were motivated by sanitary concerns. These laws deal with quadrupeds, fish, birds, and insects (Lev. 11:1–27; Deut. 14:3–21). For quadrupeds, only those that have parted hoofs and chew the cud are edible. The camel, the rock badger, the hare, and the swine are specifically rejected by name (Lev. 11:4–8; Deut. 14:8). It is specifically stated that swine's flesh is an abomination (Isa. 65:4; 66:3, 17).

Of fish, those having fins and scales are edible (Lev. 11:9–12). Of birds, a list of twenty are specified that are to be rejected (11:13–19). Of insects, the ones that have legs and leap may be eaten. The locust and grasshopper are specifically mentioned as being edible, while other flying, swarming, and crawling things are rejected (11:20–23). Distinctions in food broke down in times of want (Ezek. 4:13).

Jesus is said to have done away with distinctions concerning foods (Mk. 7:19; cf. Acts 10:12–15). These were regulations of the old covenant that have lost their significance (Heb. 9:10) and cannot confirm the faith (13:9). The effort to try to connect these regulations of the law with modern laws of hygiene breaks down when applied in details.

Water

With water being essential for human existence, as well as for animals and plants (Isa. 1:30; 55:10), early civilizations developed and were able to flourish where the rainfall was sufficient to support crops and animals

The Struthion Pool in Jerusalem, built prior to NT times, collected rainwater for the temple.

Todd Bolen/www.BiblePlaces.com

Long water channel in Megiddo dating to the Iron Age.

as well as humans, or where rain-fed rivers like the Euphrates, Tigris, and Nile flowed continuously. The establishment of permanent habitation away from the Fertile Crescent and away from the Nile relied heavily on the availability of usable underground water: natural springs (cf. Deut. 8:7) feeding streams were important for larger centers of habitation, and wells (cf. Gen. 26:18) were vital to those keeping animals.

The siting of cities like Jerusalem and Jericho had defense and water supply as major considerations. In the case of Jerusalem, to be described as the world's most significant city (Ps. 87:2–5) and the dwelling place of God (1 Ki. 8:13), the existence of the Gihon spring in the immediately adjacent Kidron Valley (2 Chr. 32:30; Isa. 7:3) was vital. In the case of the strategic city of Jericho — on the crossroads of trade and important in the protection of the Judean hill country and the Jordan Valley from invasion from the east and south (Josh. 6) — there is a copious spring in an otherwise inhospitable region.

The availability of water has been at the heart of the constant conflict, throughout the history of the Near East, of the tillers of ground and keepers of sheep (cf. Gen. 4:2). With the progressive increase of agriculture in any region, the nomadic herdsmen have been forced out of regions with reliable water supplies. In keeping with the slaying of Abel by Cain (4:8), these nomadic peoples have consistently harried the settled people, with any hydraulic works being prime targets. And the herdsmen have fought among themselves for the ownership of wells (26:20).

Not surprisingly, water has been linked with bread as necessities of human existence (1 Sam. 25:11; 1 Ki. 18:4), and the giving or withholding of these was considered to be of great importance (Deut. 23:4; Matt. 10:42). The provision of water was recognized as a divine gift. Divine blessing is spoken of in terms of water (Isa. 44:3; Jn. 4:13), and both the paucity of and the desire for spiritual life are described in terms of thirst for water (Amos 8:11; Matt. 5:6; Jn. 4:10–15). Both the common custom of carrying water to the household (Mk. 14:13) and the way in which water was drunk (Jdg. 7:5–6) were used as signs, while the common custom of washing feet (Gen. 43:24) was used by Jesus as a means of teaching (Jn. 13:5–9) and as an indicator of attitudes (Lk. 7:37, 38, 44). The use of water in religious ritual was widespread both in OT and NT times (e.g., Exod. 29:4; Lev. 15:12; Mk. 1:5, 9).

Health and Illnesses

The view that history books give of conquering and defeated armies is often a distorted one. Behind these conquests there was often a health situation that determined the outcome of wars. The nations round about Israel were deeply steeped in idolatry, and they frequently blamed their diseases on evil spirits, which must be driven out by incantations or magical formulas. Epidemics wrought havoc among these peoples, often causing them to flee their lands to get away from supposed evil spirits to which they attributed disease.

In striking contrast, the Israelites enjoyed comparatively good health. And in light of the fact that Moses was instructed in all the wisdom of the Egyptians (Acts 7:22), it is remarkable that their fanciful remedies do not appear in the Pentateuch. Nevertheless, the Bible does give some information about various diseases that affected the nation of Israel. Although most of the descriptions are general in character and simply mention the symptoms (e.g., fever, itch, sore), these illnesses appear largely to have been entities that are well known, and as a whole identical with those that now exist, especially in semitropical climates like that of Palestine.

The term *leprosy* ("Hansen's disease"), as defined today, is the name for disease processes caused by the microorganism *Mycobacterium leprae*. The Hebrew word *ṣâraʿat*, translated "leprosy" by the KJV (e.g., Lev. 13:2–3), includes a variety of skin diseases, and most scholars now believe that it does not cover true leprosy, for the relevant biblical passages make no reference to the deformity associated with this disease.

Syphilis is thought by some to be the disease called the "boils of Egypt" in Deut. 28:27. From time to time throughout the ages, syphilis has burst forth in virulent form with high mortality (cf. Num. 25:9). It is chiefly spread by sexual intercourse and is often associated with gonorrhea (cf. the "bodily discharge" in Lev. 22:4).

Smallpox, uncontrolled, has been a serious scourge throughout history until very recent times. It consists of red spots that turn rapidly into blisterlike pustules over the entire body, including the face. Some have suggested that Job's "sores" (Job 2:7) were actually smallpox. The Hebrew word here, however, may indicate several other types of diseased skin, such as a pustule or a boil. Hezekiah's illness (2 Ki. 20:7), which was almost fatal, may well have been a true boil or carbuncle. Another suggestion is that it was anthrax.

Festering boils are recorded among the plagues of Egypt (Exod. 9:9). This disease has provoked much speculation and two alternative explanations. (a) Since both man and beast were infected with virtually the same disease, it may have been smallpox in humans and cowpox in cattle. (b) The "terrible" fifth plague (9:3) was anthrax of animals, later transmitted to humans as malignant pustule. Untreated, anthrax is a fatal infectious disease, chiefly of cattle and sheep, characterized by the formation of hard lumps and ulcers and symptoms of collapse. Without modern therapy it is often fatal.

Scabies is called "the itch, from which you cannot be cured" (Deut. 28:27). It is caused by a tiny insect allied to spiders that burrows under the skin. The itching is intense. Infection is spread to others through close bodily contact. The ancients knew no cure for it, but it readily responds to modern medicines.

Bubonic plague begins with fever and chills that are followed by prostration, delirium, headache, vomiting, and diarrhea. This disease apparently broke out among the Philistines when they placed the captured ark of the covenant in an idol temple (1 Sam. 5). This disease is transmitted by rats through infected fleas that they carry on their bodies, the fleas transferring to humans for livelihood after the rat host dies of the disease. The disease causes the lymph nodes of the groin and armpits to enlarge to the size of walnuts. These enlarged nodes are known as buboes (KJV, "emerods"; NIV, "tumors"). This outbreak of bubonic plague was attributed to "rats that are destroying the country" (6:5).

Tuberculosis occurs in acute or chronic form, more commonly the latter. Under the living conditions of OT days, it probably not only attacked the lungs (a common form in America today), but also the bones and joints (common in underdeveloped lands today). "Crookback" (cf. the extreme hunchback of Lev. 21:20) may result from tuberculosis of the spinal vertebrae or less commonly from severe back injury. The disease may produce chronic invalidism or death if the disease process is not arrested.

Malaria may have been the "high fever" with which Peter's mother-in-law was stricken (Lk. 4:38; cf. also Lev. 26:16; Deut. 28:22). Transmitted by certain species of mosquito, malaria is responsible for much chronic illness. A chill followed by fever often subsides in a few hours only to recur more severely some hours later, continuing intermittently thereafter. Death may follow if the disease is not treated.

Diarrhea, dysentery, and *cholera*, caused by microorganisms taken into the body in contaminated food or drink, were doubtless prevalent in OT times. They are characterized by frequent watery bowel movements, often by vomiting and fever, and if protracted, by weakness and prostration. Publius's father's illness (Acts 28:8) is rightly understood by modern versions to have been fever and dysentery, a diarrhea associated with painful spasms of the bowel, ulceration, and infection. Some think that dysentery destroyed Sennacherib's army (2 Ki. 19:35) when 185,000 men were all "dead bodies" by early morning.

Intestinal roundworm infection (ascariasis) is a common disease today in lands where sanitation is poor and is believed to have been responsible for Herod Agrippa I's death (Acts 12:21–23). The pinkish yellow roundworm, *Ascaris lumbricoides*, is about 10–16 inches long. Aggregated worms sometimes form a tight ball with their interlocking bodies so as to obstruct the intestine, producing severe pain and copious vomiting of worms. If the obstruction is not promptly relieved by surgery, death may ensue. The roundworm does not chew and devour, but feeds on the nutrient fluids in the bowel and may work its way through diseased portions of the bowel as though it had eaten a hole through it. The account of Agrippa's death by the Jewish historian Josephus (*Antiquities of the Jews* 19.8.2 §§343–52) is highly suggestive of the intestinal obstruction produced by these worms.

The *snakebite* that Paul received was doubtless inflicted by a venomous snake of the pit-viper type (Acts 28:3–6). When envenomation by this snake takes place, the tissues may quickly swell to three or four times their normal size in the region of the bite.

Trachoma is an infectious eye disease, very common in ancient times. Early in the disease there is often acute inflammation of the eyelids, which makes the lids feel like sandpaper. This frequently spreads on to the bulb of the eye, especially the cornea, the transparent part of the bulb, which becomes red and inflamed. At this state, infection with other germs is often added. Pus seeps out over the lid margins, forming a tough, crusting scab as it dries and unites with the greasy secretion of the glands of the lid margin. Many have speculated that trachoma was the illness Paul suffered when he first visited Galatia (Gal. 4:13–15; perhaps the same as the "thorn in my flesh" of 2 Cor. 12:7). Some even suggest that Paul's blindness encountered on the Damascus road (Acts 9:8–9, 17–19) was of this type. Numerous other interpretations, including malaria and epilepsy, have been proposed.

Nervous and mental diseases. We read in Prov. 17:22, "A cheerful heart is good medicine, / but a crushed spirit dries up the bones." In ancient times, as today, pressure and anxiety can have a serious effect on one's physical condition. In addition, there are mental and emotional problems that are recognized as disease entities just as distinctive as appendicitis or pneumonia. The general term used in KJV for those so afflicted is "lunatic," though formerly this term referred to epilepsy as well as insanity because of a supposed relationship to the phases of the moon. As today, legal responsibility for actions was tempered by proof of mental incompetence. Hence we find David escaping from Achish by pretending "insanity" (cf. 1 Sam. 21:13–15). Perhaps he was even imitating some of Saul's actions (cf. 16:15–23; 19:9–10). The modern psychiatrist would diagnose Saul's state as *manic-depressive insanity*, with its periods of black melancholy, flashes of homicidal violence, and deeply rooted delusion that people were plotting against him, characteristically ending in Saul's suicide. Nebuchadnezzar (Dan. 4:24–28) is thought by some to have been a victim of paranoia, a delusional form of insanity well known to medical science.

The woman's *issue of blood* (NIV, "bleeding") of twelve years' duration (Lk. 8:43–44) was doubtless excessive menstrual flow, a fairly common condition. In its severe form, it is commonly due to fibroid tumors in the womb encroaching on the lining of the womb. A flow of blood with large clots occurs, depleting the body of blood and causing severe anemia. The modern remedy typically used in this condition is removal of the tumor from the womb or removal of the womb (hysterectomy). This surgery obviously was not available in NT times, so it is quite understandable that all of this woman's living was spent on unsuccessful medical care.

Gangrene. Timothy was admonished to shun profane babblings because "their teaching will spread like gangrene" (2 Tim. 2:17). The term refers to local death of the tissues. Common forms of gangrene are (a) gas gangrene, a rapidly fatal type caused by a spreading gas-forming germ in muscles after recent injury; (b) diabetic gangrene, a "dry" gangrene that spreads less rapidly caused by circulatory impairment associated with uncontrolled diabetes; and (c) septic

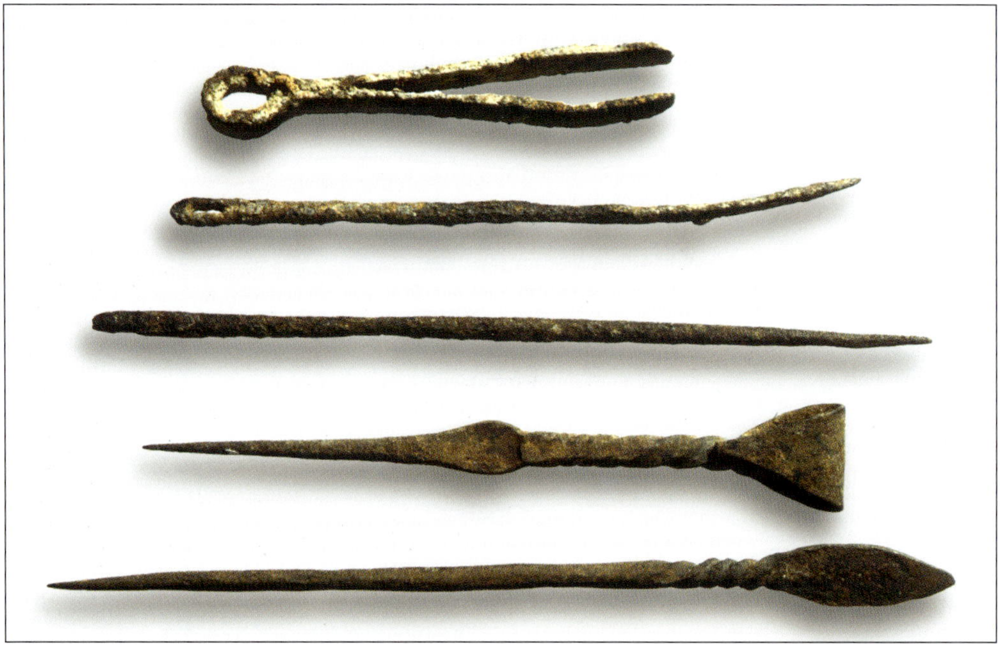

Roman surgical instruments.

Z. Radovan/www.BibleLandPictures.com

gangrene that spreads from the edges of infected ulcers.

Dropsy (Lk. 14:2), in modern medical language called *edema,* is a condition in which the tissues retain too much fluid. It may be caused by heart disease, kidney disease, or local infection and may terminate fatally.

Dwarfism is referred to in Lev. 21:20. People may have been dwarfed through tuberculosis or injury of the spine, but deficiency of thyroid function such as is found in cretinism is also a likely cause. In the latter condition there is also usually mental deficiency, and this gives added reason for not permitting such an individual to participate in priestly service. Cretinism today responds well to thyroid extract therapy if administered early in life.

Various *orthopedic* conditions are mentioned, as when reference is made to the *maimed* (those whose bodies are deprived of a part) and the *halt* (those who limp in walking because of lameness from a disabled lower extremity). The latter may be due to a fracture that has healed in an unfavorable position or it may be due to *atrophy* (wasting) of the muscles. Atrophy of a hand is referred to as a "shriveled" hand in Lk. 6:6 (KJV, "withered"). Atrophy usually results from *palsy* or *paralysis* (synonymous terms), a condition characterized by loss of control of movement of muscles through disease or destruction of nerves or nervous tissue.

Muteness, that is, inability to speak, may arise from deafness since one will naturally find it difficult to reproduce unheard sounds. It also may arise from hemorrhage (apoplexy) or thrombosis (clotting) in relation to the blood vessels of one or more of the speech centers of the brain. Often a marked degree of recovery takes place in these instances of so-called stroke as the clotted blood is gradually absorbed from the affected area. Nabal (1 Sam. 25:36–38) evidently experienced a fatal stroke.

How did the Israelites deal with these illnesses? Because of ceremonial concerns regarding ritual purity, priests functioned as health consultants in diagnosing diseases (Lev. 13–14), but very little is said about medical treatments. There is occasional mention of natural remedies, such as a balm native to Gilead that evidently had medicinal properties (Jer. 46:11; cf. also 2 Ki. 20:7). The few references to physicians in the OT suggest that they were not held in high regard (2 Chr. 16:12; Job 13:4; Jer. 8:22; cf. also Lk. 4:23; 8:43). Inadequate medical help made the Hebrews very conscious of their need to depend on God for healing (Exod. 15:26; Ps. 103:3; Jer. 30:17).

In the NT, James urges that the church elders be called to pray for the sick. He also directs that they "anoint them with oil in the name of the Lord" (Jas. 5:14). Some believe that this directive refers to a church ritual, so that the oil is symbolic of miraculous healing. The verb *anoint*, however, commonly referred to rubbing olive oil on the skin as a household remedy. James probably means that the sick one is not only to be prayed for, but that the commonly accepted remedies are also to be applied as an indication of compassionate concern. Jesus' disciples made similar use of the application of oil to the sick (Mk. 6:13).

Alabaster bottles contained perfumes or other ointments.

Chapter 3

Work

God's original purpose for human beings is expressed in the Bible under the divine commission to Adam that he should work the ground and thus take care of the garden of Eden (Gen. 2:15). This divine purpose finds its highest expression in the responsibility given to human beings to "subdue" and "rule" the created natural order (1:28).

Cultivation

Agriculture — the work of cultivating plants and caring for livestock — is fundamental to civilization, for it enables the farmer to produce surplus food that frees others for specialized occupations. Israel's agriculture was typical of the countries in the ancient Near East. The crops produced, with emphasis upon cereal grains, were those common to the Fertile Crescent. Ecological factors in the Holy Land caused variation in pattern and emphasis, with certain adaptations reflected in techniques and production.

Although the Hebrews were a pastoral people during the Egyptian sojourn (Gen.

This wall painting from an Egyptian tomb (c. 15th cent. BC) depicts men making wine and performing other types of labor.

47:6), they undoubtedly became familiar with Egyptian agriculture, which was strongly correlated with the annual flooding rhythm of the Nile. The Egyptian farming system was based on natural and artificial irrigation for the production of grains, fruits, and vegetables. When occupying the Promised Land, the Hebrews necessarily adopted Canaanite farming methods in the transition from pastoralism to agriculture.

In addition, the Israelites would have known Mesopotamian farming methods through cultural contacts accompanying trade and conquest. The ecological pattern in the Tigris-Euphrates Valley differed from the Nile Valley, for Mesopotamian flooding was erratic and disastrous, with consequent flood control and an extensive canal system. Nevertheless, both lands produced similar crops, especially grains, by irrigation. The Israelites grew the same crops but could not employ the same irrigation techniques in the hill-and-valley complex of the Holy Land.

The land of Palestine is predominantly hilly. The precipitous slopes along the Jordan Rift Valley prevent cultivation except in narrow valley floors or where terracing is practical. The northern uplands west of the Jordan Valley are characterized by hills interspersed with several valleys of sufficient area to favor agriculture. To the south in Judea's hill lands the area is largely in slope, where terracing and a few undulating hill crests between Jerusalem and Beersheba permit field cultivation. South of the Judean massif the terrain slopes gradually into the Negev, where aridity restricts farming more than does the terrain. The Plain of Sharon west of Samaria is largely arable. The plateau east of the Jordan begins precipitously from the valley, but the crest area (Bashan, Gilead, Ammon, and Moab) is admirably suited to cultivation.

Palestine is only about one-fourth the size of Iowa, and so its climatic diversity is surprising. Rainfall is much more abundant and dependable in the north, where the highlands receive thirty inches annually, than in the Beersheba area to the south, where half that amount falls with much annual irregularity. Moreover, easterly moving cyclonic storms deposit heavier rainfall on the higher western slopes in contrast to the arid "rain shadow" slopes facing east. The western exposure of Judea averages over twenty inches annually, but the Dead Sea, a few miles east, gets less than five inches. Rainfall occurs during the cool season, the "early rains" beginning in October and the "latter rains" falling during March and April. In biblical days the agricultural cycle corresponded with the alternating wet and dry seasons: the farmers planted their all-important grain fields at the inception of the rainfall and harvested when the rainy season ended.

The nature of the soil too is quite varied. Some of the larger valleys and the Plain of Sharon have fertile soils formed from deep alluvium, but in the highlands and the arid sections the soil is thin, less developed, and stony. In ancient Philistia and the Beersheba area, several inches of loess formed fertile soils, but aridity limited production. The hilly soils of Judah, Ephraim, Ammon, and Moab are thin and stony, but there is fertility, since they develop from limestone into calcareous types. Galilee, Bashan, and Gilead soils are also productive, for they are "recently" formed from underlying basalt. Of course, the soils are thinnest on steep slopes, and the farmer usually clears many stones from these fields to be used for fences or terrace walls.

Grapevines north of Hebron.

Todd Bolen/www.BiblePlaces.com

Israel's major agricultural products are summarized in 2 Chr. 2:15: "Now let my Lord send his servants the wheat and barley and the olive oil and wine he promised." These were the staple items in the people's diet; hence most farmers attempted to produce as many of them as possible. However, the environmental diversity favored production of one crop in certain areas, with other crops secondary to the dominant one. Judah led in viticulture, for the grape vine enjoyed a favorable ecological niche in the sunny terraced hillsides. To the north in Ephraim (or Samaria) the limestone weathered into a fertile *terra rossa* soil that, coupled with adequate rainfall, proved to be the setting par excellence for the olive tree. Farther north, the open valleys of Galilee, with rich alluvium soils and ample rainfall, favored extensive wheat production; this was true also of Bashan, east of the Jordan. To the south near the Negev and in Philistia, the loessial soils were fertile, but rainfall was scanty, so barley was predominant.

Israelite farmers started their annual cycle with the olive harvest from mid-September to mid-November. The leading task during this period was picking the olives and extracting their oil for multiple uses. Of course olive trees need attention, so the farmer, to insure high productivity, plowed the soil around the trees in the spring to eliminate weeds and to create a surface mulch for retaining subsurface moisture for the trees during the rainless summer months. Pruning was also a spring chore to prevent excessive shoots from parasitic drain on the tree and thus reduce yield. The tree blossomed in May with the small white flowers falling a few days after opening (Job 15:33).

The berries developed during the summer and began to ripen in September, when the first ripe berries dropped before the farmer and his family began picking. Long sticks were used to dislodge most berries, but agile youths often climbed the trees to procure the uppermost berries. The immature olives were left to ripen and be gathered later by the destitute (Deut. 24:20). Some olives were pickled in brine to be eaten with bread, but oil was more important and extracted in a number of ways. A simple method was to crush the berries by hand in a bowl-shaped stone that had a channel to convey the oil into a receptacle. A larger operation was to crush the berries in a stone vat with the feet, but the most efficient method used by those caring for sizable orchards was to transport the fruit on basket-laden donkeys to mills where crushing was accomplished by a circular millstone. Besides multiple dietary uses, the oil served as medication (Lk. 10:34) and for anointing, the latter having symbolical implications of peace and prosperity (Ps. 23:5).

With the inception of the "early rains" in November, the farmer began plowing the fields preparatory to sowing the cereal grains. Agriculture among the Israelites was characterized by the field type of cultivation with plow and draft animals (usually oxen). The shape of the fields tended to be rectangular to accommodate the linear furrows of the plow; the size of the fields depended on the terrain, and the area under cultivation in a given year corresponded to the area that could be plowed.

The typical plow was constructed of wood with a copper or bronze plowpoint until the Israelites acquired iron for points from the Philistines in the tenth century BC. These plows are not to be confused with contemporary steel plows, which have shares and moldboards for completely turning six or more inches of soil. The ancient plow scratched the surface to a depth of three or four inches without covering weeds or stubble. This plow with its wooden beam attached to a yoke of oxen may be observed even today in Middle Eastern countries.

Although a seeder was attached to some plows in ancient Mesopotamia, whereby the seeds were channeled from a hopper through a tube to be deposited behind the plowpoint, the Israelites apparently did not adopt the implement. Sowing was by a broadcast method, with the farmer casting the seed with sweeping actions of the hand and arm as he trudged up and down the field. The seed was carried in a basket or in a pouch attached to the waist. The grain was covered promptly by a second plowing or by dragging branches or a log behind oxen. This method of "harrowing" served to level the field, to cover the seed to insure germination, and to prevent birds from eating the seed (Isa. 28:24–25; Matt. 13:4). The farmer usually selected the most fertile fields for wheat and less favorable sites for barley, lentils, or spelt.

The grain sowing continued until January, when the "late planting" of other crops occurred. These supplementary crops included millet, sesame, chick peas, lentils, melons, cucumbers, garlic, and other vegetables. Customarily the vegetables were raised in garden plots near the village and farmer's home. Sowing grain was men's work, but women aided in planting and caring for the gardens. These planting and weeding activities continued into March.

The rainfall declined in April as the barley began to ripen, with barley reaping at its height in May. After the barley had

Very ancient wooden plow with blade.

Steve Gorton © Dorling Kindersley

Wheat.

© Odelia Cohen/www.BigStockPhoto.com

been reaped, the farmers began wheat harvest, which continued into June. To reap the grain, they used small sickles with which they severed the stalks gathered in handfuls with the free hand (Ps. 129:7). Farmers owning much livestock cut the stalks close to the ground to increase the supply of straw for fodder and bedding purposes. Those who had no livestock cut the stalks within a few inches of the heads ("ears") of grain so there was less straw to interfere with threshing.

As the reapers cut the grain, the stalks were gathered into unbound sheaths to facilitate carrying the grain to the threshing floor. A division of labor prevailed in the harvest fields, with men cutting the grain, children aiding in gathering it into sheaths, and women gleaning for stray stalks, as dramatically portrayed in the book of Ruth. Rain seldom fell during the harvest season, therefore little spoilage occurred. Two major threats to a bountiful harvest confronted the farmer, however: the dreaded hot wind ("sirocco") from the desert occasionally withered the ripening kernels, or an invasion of locusts might consume much of the crop.

The reaped grain was carried and stacked on threshing floors near the villages. These threshing floors were either a circular area on a flat outcropping of rock or an area about forty feet in diameter that was cleared of stones, leveled, moistened, and packed so that the surface was sun-baked and hard. In threshing, the sheaves were pitched on the floor to be trampled by oxen drawing a sledge on which the farmer rode. The oxen hoofs and the sharp studs embedded in the underside of the sledge separated the kernels from the straw and chaff while reducing the straw into bits. Some farmers preferred a disk-harrow implement rather than the sledge; this implement was likewise drawn by oxen and was superior to the sledge in that not as many kernels were crushed (Isa. 28:27–28).

After the grain had been reduced to a mass of kernels, chaff, and chopped straw, the winnowing followed. Using a pitchfork with closely spaced tines, the farmer tossed the mass repeatedly in the air to expose it to the wind that carried the chaff and straw away. The opportune time for winnowing was toward evening, when the daily sea breeze provided a steady, but not too strong, flow of air. Customarily the threshed grain remained in heaps on the threshing floor with someone sleeping near the grain to prevent theft (Ruth 3). Later the grain was bagged for carrying it to storage in large jars or, in some cases, put in plastered silos that had been excavated beneath the floor of wealthy homes. Since rent and taxes were

A man winnowing grain to remove the chaff.

commonly paid in kind, some grain was transported by donkey to large pit silos built by wealthy landowners or the government.

Caring for the vine became the farmer's preoccupation following grain harvest. The vine required attention earlier in the spring in the "latter rain" period. Each spring the farmer removed stones from the vineyard, repaired terrace walls, pruned the dead branches, and plowed or harrowed the ground about the vines to create a moisture-retaining mulch and destroy weeds. As the grapes formed and ripened, they required constant attention to prevent loss to wild animals (Cant. 2:15). The farmer, or a hired watchman, stationed himself in a tower built especially for this purpose, permitting surveillance of many vineyards.

When picking time arrived in August and September, the entire family frequently moved into a temporary shelter ("booth") where they lived while picking the grapes. While some grapes were eaten fresh and some were preserved in dried form as raisins, most of the grapes were reduced to juice to allow fermentation into wine. An air of festivity prevailed during the grape harvest and accompanying activity at the wine presses (Isa. 16:10). The common method of extracting grape juice was by placing the grapes in the upper end of a wide stone receptacle where they were crushed under foot with the juice draining into a basin at the lower end of the receptacle.

Figs, picked also at the close of summer, ranked as a staple in the people's diet (Deut. 8:8). The antiquity of the fig is suggested by the narrative of Adam and Eve, who are said to have converted fig leaves into aprons (Gen. 3:7). The fig tree extended productivity because it thrived in rugged stony terrain unsuited for most other important food plants. A slow-growing tree requiring many years to bear substantially, the fig became symbolic of economic and political continuity and stability in the land (1 Ki. 4:25).

Yielding two crops annually, the fig tree produced the first crop in June from midsummer sprouts from the previous year, but the second crop in August was more important. The fruit generally was dried and pressed into cakes for later consumption, and its high sugar content, together with the date, was a main source of sugar in Israel's diet. The fig cakes were used also for medicinal purposes, as in the remarkable healing of Hezekiah (2 Ki. 20:7).

Pomegranate trees, like fig trees, are deciduous and put forth leaves as well as brilliant scarlet blossoms in April. The tree requires little attention, and the fruit ripens in September when it is picked. The agricultural cycle each year concluded with the pomegranate harvest.

Livestock

The Israelites entered the Promised Land as a pastoral people with cultural traditions extending back to Abraham, the pastoral nomad (Gen. 13). After possessing Canaan, they experienced a transition from pastoralism to agriculture, which they adopted from the sedentary Canaanites. However, livestock persisted in their economic activities and contributed to the cultural ethos for a number of reasons. Much of the land was not arable but was admirably suited to herding (1 Sam. 16:11; Amos 1:1). Not only did animals provide products and income for the rural dweller, but it is clear that ceremonial rites in worship emphasized animal sacrifice in the tabernacle and temple services (1 Ki. 8:5; Heb. 9:18–22).

Cattle being used for agricultural purposes.

Shepherd with a lamb in the Negev.

Todd Bolen/www.BiblePlaces.com

The common domesticated animals in Israel included sheep, goats, cattle, donkeys, and dogs. Camels, of course, should be included, but they were not kept by the typical farmer, for they did not fit economically into a sedentary pattern of life; therefore, camel owners were usually tradesmen or desert nomads. Horses seem to have been prestigious animals and a luxury in which most farmers could not indulge; they were used primarily for chariots and cavalry in the king's military system. Donkeys were beasts of burden and carried both people and products, much as they continue to do in undeveloped rural areas of contemporary Middle Eastern countries (cf. Matt. 21:5). Cattle or oxen were also beasts of burden, since they drew the plow, harrow, and other farming implements, and they were used for sacrificial purposes. They do not seem to have been kept for milk or meat products as in Western culture.

Sheep were the most important animals to ancient Israelites and are mentioned early in the biblical record (Gen. 4:2). The fat-tailed variety, still popular in the Middle East, was preferred, since the heavy tail, with its store of fat, enabled the sheep to tolerate uncertain grazing conditions during periods of drought. Mutton was favored as the source of meat, and wool was spun and woven into cloth for garments. They played the major role in sacrificial offerings. The typical Israelite herd included goats with the sheep, for goats provided several products: meat, hair for a coarse cloth and tenting material (the tent made of black goat hair is traditional in Bible lands and is still used by bedouins and other nomads), skins for bottles used for storing wine or carrying water and other liquids, and milk (these bottles were the preferred type among the people).

It may be noted that sheep and goats were far more common in Israel due to their greater tolerance of marginal grazing conditions than cattle and horses. The keeping of sheep and other aspects of shepherd life are used as illustrations for spiritual relationships, with the shepherd as a great metaphor for the Lord and his care (Ps. 23; Jn. 10).

Woodworking

Ancient Palestine was heavily forested and, because of its diverse climate, had a very wide variety of timber. Woodworkers recognized the virtues of different woods and used them according to their properties. Olive wood, for example, was ideal for carving, so the cherubim of Solomon's temple were carved from that wood (1 Ki. 6:23); the holm oak, on the other hand, made the best plow for a farmer.

After felling a tree, workers had to cut it up into usable units. If boards were to be made, the trunk sections had to be rip-sawed into boards; it was a tricky task to keep the boards of equal width, but these workers were specialists. Larger units as beams could be shaped with an adze from tree sections that were approximately the size of the beam desired.

The carpenter worked only on certain sections of the stone or mud-brick house. Timber was too expensive to be used for an entire house, since everything had to be hand-sawed. The carpenter fashioned the doors and frames, the latticed windows, and the window frames. He also made the fine latticed wood screens used in wealthy

Man using carpentry tools.

Todd Bolen/www.BiblePlaces.com. Used by permisssion of Nazareth Village. www.nazarethvillage.com

homes. If the house had a second story he would put in that floor and perhaps some paneling. If the house used wooden columns he would shape these but would plant them on a wide stone base. Stairs were made of wood or stone.

If there was a yard around a wealthy home, carpenters would make the gate, whose keys might be of wood or metal. The carpenter would also make furniture for the poor, but the rich would want a cabinet maker. A beautiful dining room set might be made by an Arab cabinet maker, who used only fine tools. A minimum of furniture for the rich would be beds, chairs, stools, tables, and chests for the storing of clothes. Royalty would need a still better craftsman for the building of thrones, footstools, etc. Special craftsmen would work on the bone and ivory inlaid furniture.

Probably one craftsman in wood specialized in the making of wooden items used by the farmer. He would make yokes, plows, ox goads, pitchforks, shovels, threshing sledges, and perhaps a hay wagon. (A wagon took extra skill because of the wheels.) This woodworker also probably made the wooden frames for the pack saddles used on donkeys and camels. One of the most skilled workers was the man who made and repaired chariots, for he worked on the axle of wheels, the bed, and the tongue. The metalworker fashioned the rim. A skilled craftsman made the litter on which the rich would ride.

There was a woodworker who specialized in the making of weapons, furnishing the wood parts. He made the bow and the arrows, as well as the shafts for spear, javelin, and mace. The mace often served as a scepter. He constructed the catapult and the beam for the battering ram, as well as the housing for it, and made the assault towers and other siege engines.

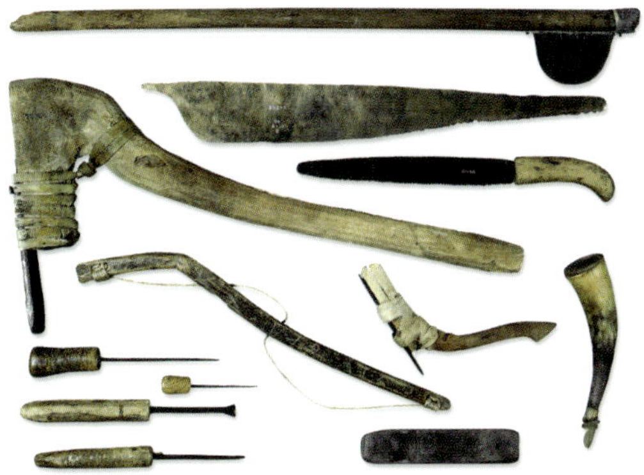

The tools of a carpenter.

Shipping included several special trades in the field of woodworking. The timber must be cut and fashioned to fit the hull, and one or two masts shaped and set in place. Oars were normal emergency power, and the ship was steered by special oars as rudders. If the ship was large, it would have been decked over. The ship's caulker with his pitch, bitumen, wool, and tow worked hand in hand with the ship carpenter.

Someone made prison equipment such as stocks and gibbets and crosses. Some delicate woodworker made the beams for scales and balances. Skill was required by those who carved dolls (and idols) and fashioned wooden keys. Finally, the woodworker in turn had specialists to make his metal tools and other specialists to furnish him with whetstones, emery, chalk, string, etc.

Quarrying and Metallurgy

Public buildings and wealthy homes needed good building stone. Most of Palestine could furnish limestone, while southern Transjordan (e.g., Moab) had sandstone. Northern Transjordan has basalt, but this is not a beautiful stone, although it was widely used

Craftsman stone mason at the temple of Karnak in Luxor, Egypt.
© Robert Harding Picture Library Ltd/Alamy

there. Some Palestine marble was doubtless used as is done today.

Quarrying is a profession of its own. The best stone was reserved for the Jerusalem temples. A great underground quarry lies under a part of the old city of Jerusalem, and the marks of the quarry worker are everywhere. It may well have been the source of stone for Solomon's temple. The tools used in this profession are the metal chisel, baskets, wooden wedges, water to spread the wedges, and wooden rollers for the largest stones. The transport of the stone might have been done by the quarry owner, the user, or a third party. Long-distance hauling would have been by camel and donkey.

The stone mason fashioned wine vats, olive presses, and the weights used in them, and vats for the fuller and dyer. Stone water pots are mentioned in the NT (Jn. 2:6). Masons made tombstones for Rachel (Gen. 35:20) and memorial pillars for Absalom (2 Sam. 18:18). Other workers in stone made the saddle querns and riders and all varieties of mortars and pestles, slingshot stones, and weights of all sizes and from many varieties

Ancient depiction of Egyptians working metal.

Z. Radovan/www.BibleLandPictures.com

of stones. The bottom of the metal workers' bellow was a specially fashioned stone.

More careful work was done in the rouge palettes and alabaster vases for perfumes. The most skilled craftsmen worked in scarabs, seal cylinders, and stamp seals. The heathen stonemason worked on the "pillars," the idols, and their altars. Lime for the mason's mortar was made by workers who ran the lime kilns.

Salt and brimstone as well as lye and pigments could be handled by the quarry method. Flint was taken from a quarry, and flint-working was a craft of its own. Flint tools and weapons were common in Abraham's day. The flint sickle edge was used all through the OT. In one sense a clay bed could be a quarry, but the removal of the clay would be done by a potter's apprentice. Many precious stones such as turquoise also came from the quarry worker.

The copper ores of Palestine were worked on an international scale as far back as the days of Abraham, and much earlier than that. Genesis 14 recorded a war whose prize was the copper mines of Edom and Sinai. The mines could be open-face or consist of chambers and tunnel. Much of the labor seems to have been done by slaves or prisoners of war. The tools of the quarry workers were used also by the miners, but they needed additional ones, such as stone mortars and stone pestles, because the ores had to be crushed. There were also quern types of stone used for crushing the ore. Baskets carried crushed ore to the smelters.

Smelting was a skilled profession, and Palestine smelters often did excellent work

Copper mine from the Calcolithic (Copper) Age in the Timna Valley, southern Israel.

Todd Bolen/www.BiblePlaces.com

This bronze mirror with ivory handle dates to the 14th cent. BC.
Todd Bolen/www.BiblePlaces.com

with the tools available. They needed furnaces (usually stone and clay) and leather bellows to furnish sufficient air draft. Charcoal was the best fuel, furnished by Edom's forests for the mines in the Arabah below. Wooden poles had to be introduced into the molten metal. Various chemical reagents were needed to be mixed with the ores in order to extract the copper and separate it from the dross discard. The smelted ore was poured out into ingots of various sizes and shapes. The ore would be refined again later in better grades of furnaces. Some of these types of furnaces have been discovered by the archaeologists. As mines and smelters in Edom and Sinai were far removed from civilization, temporary quarters were erected for the workmen, many of them slaves, who probably worked primarily in the winter season.

The Philistines were the first to introduce iron into Palestine, and they held a monopoly on its working. Iron works quite differently from copper. It is unknown when Palestine first mined and smelted its own iron ore. In Gilead one cave mine with ore of very rich content has been found, and the ore from it was smelted at the cave's mouth. Smelting iron was a much more difficult task than that for copper.

The metal worker took the ingot and worked it up into tools, weapons, jewelry, and any use for which there was a demand. For common work the coppersmith melted the ingot and poured it into stone or pottery molds of open or closed type. If the metal needed reshaping this could be done by hammering, which also hardened the metal. Copper could be cold-worked or hot-worked. If a harder metal and a sharper cutting edge was needed, tin was added to the copper to make bronze. Bronze, however, was quite expensive. Long before the time of Abraham the metal workers of the ancient Near East had succeeded in doing almost everything with copper and its alloys that could be done even in modern times (until new technologies were developed in the twentieth century AD).

The blacksmith had to work his metal hot, and that craft demanded real skill. Iron demanded heavier tools in anvils, hammers, and tongs than copper. Iron working used a great deal of good-grade charcoal; iron did not come into mass production in Palestine until the time of David. Since iron rusted quickly in the wet climate of Palestine, the archaeologist must go to dry Egypt to get well-preserved iron tools for his metallurgical studies.

Most of the tool types were the same whether the metal was copper or iron: axes and adzes, hoes, mattocks, and shovels, plus plowshares, chisels, and knives. Knives in particular were in wide varieties because of their multiple uses and the materials that they cut. There were braces and drills of many kinds, bits, augers and awls, planes and drawing knives, anvils, hammers and tongs, mortar rake and trowel, plum-line, level, and square. There were saws for wood, stone, and metal, files and rasps, sickles and pruning hooks, also rings and nails, pins, needles, scissors, etc. Chariots and wagons needed metal tires for the wheels. Weights and scale pans often were metal. Coins always were made of metal.

Much of the military equipment required metal. Copper, bronze, or iron was used in the following military equipment: spear, javelin and arrowhead, helmet, shield, and body armor with greaves; sword and dagger; mace and battle axe, etc.; even the head of the great battering ram. The army's "flag" was usually a metal standard such as Rome used. It was necessary to have chains and fetters for the prisoners of war. All of these tools and weapons came in multiple forms.

Beauty must be cultivated so there were razors and strigils, also mirrors, tweezers, brooches, and a wealth of jewelry in copper. Copper kettles and kitchen ware of all kinds were used in the homes of the rich, and copperware was used on their dining tables. Also, there was a wealth of metalwork for the heathen craftsmen who cast the molten idol and for those who fashioned the metal plates over the wooden idol core. There were many metal tools that accompanied the service of the altar.

The jeweler is worthy of special mention since jewelry was one method of holding wealth. Jewelry could at any time be converted into money because of its gold and silver content, skillfully worked to multiply its value. Precious and semiprecious stones added to its costliness. Carrying precious stones was one method of transporting great wealth in small packages.

Jewelry items included rings, necklaces, brooches, pendants, earrings, bracelets and

Gold jewelry from Tell el-ʿAjjul, mid-2nd millennium BC.

Z. Radovan/www.BibleLandPictures.com

Collection of ancient pottery bowls.

anklets, amulets, scarabs, and beads of all kinds. Palestine had no gold or silver mines, but it had excellent silversmiths and goldsmiths. The better jewelry was gold and silver. These jewelry craftsmen also worked in all varieties of precious and semiprecious stones. Cheaper jewelry was in copper and bronze. The poorest was made of bone. Some ivory work, however, was very expensive.

Pottery Making

The choice of clay used determines many features of the finished pottery. When clay is fired to the state of pottery, a completely new material is created. It was the first synthetic material invented. Pottery has several phases of work. Clay must be dug and weathered, then treaded well before use. Most of the vessels were made on the potter's wheel, but some were shaped by hand, and other pieces were made in a press mold. The firing of the ware demanded special skills.

Pottery was especially useful in the house. There were various kinds of cooking pots, griddles, and kettles for deep-fat frying. There were mixing bowls and large and small storage jars for dry foods and liquids. There was tableware of all kinds, also lamps and lampstands. There was the brazier to keep the house warm in winter; and the soldier needed a special army canteen that held cold water. There were kettles for manufacturing perfumes and many varieties of perfume juglets, etc.

In the building trades, mud was used as the cheapest mortar. Large sun-dried bricks were made in special molds. Burnt brick and enameled brick were not used in Palestine, although both were employed in Mesopotamia and Egypt. Roof tiles were used in Roman times. Clay also was shaped into stoves for cooking and ovens for baking. Clay silos were used to store grain.

The metal worker used pottery crucibles of various types, smelting furnaces, and pottery molds for the metal objects cast. Pottery spindle whorls and pottery loom weights were used in cloth industries. Among the heathen there were clay figurines and incense altars.

Glass was one phase of the ceramic industries, although it was just coming into mass production about NT times. Up to that time it was classed as luxury goods and was used especially by the perfume and mosaic industries. Faience was a related trade, but Palestine imported this ware from Egypt.

Other Occupations

Baker. This trade occupied a special street in Jerusalem (Jer. 37:21). The baking of bread was one of the chief household duties. But in the towns and principal villages, the larger oven of the regular baker is required (1 Sam. 8:13). In addition to the home and public bakers, there was the royal baker, who baked for the king (Gen. 40:1–22; 41:10). The Hebrews used large stone jars, open at the mouth, about three feet high, with a fire inside for baking

Pottery from the Copper Age (5th millennium BC).

Z. Radovan/www.BibleLandPictures.com

bread and cakes. As soon as the sides were sufficiently heated, the thin dough was applied to the outside, and the opening at the top was closed. Sometimes wood was used for heating, but more often thorns and occasionally dry dung were used (Ezek. 4:12).

Barber. Great attention was paid to the hair and beard among the ancients, so the barber must have been a well-known tradesman, though the word *barber* occurs only once in Scripture (Ezek. 5:1). Barbers may have been involved in the shaving of the head as part of a vow (Num. 6:18–19). The instruments of their work were probably the razor, the basin, the mirror, and perhaps the scissors. They usually plied their trade in the open, on the street.

Clerk. The "city clerk" at Ephesus was an official who dispersed the mob gathered at

Beautiful bichrome pottery discovered in Megiddo.

© Kim Walton

Fishermen using a dragnet.
Library of Congress, LC-DIG-matpc-05687

the theater to attack Paul (Acts 19:35). In the Greco-Roman world, such a clerk occupied a position of considerable importance in urban administration. His initial duties consisted of keeping the records of the city, taking the minutes of the council and assembly, caring for official correspondence, receiving the edicts of emperors and governors, plus a great mass of miscellaneous documents, then filing and publishing these, as required. He publicly read decrees, put up temporary notices for the people to read, and those of permanent importance were inscribed on stone.

Counselor. Advisers played a very important role, particularly with matters of state (2 Sam. 15:12; 1 Chr. 27:33). This position usually ranked them among the chief officials of the government (Ezra 4:5; Job 3:14; 12:17; Isa. 19:11).

Cupbearer. Due to the ever-present possibility of intrigue, the serving of wine was one of great responsibility and trust. The officer's chief duty was to guard the king's person. The first mention of a cupbearer is in the Joseph story (Gen. 40:2); since the man there is designated as "chief cupbearer," several must have held a similar position under him. Under Solomon, this office was apparently very important, for his cupbearers highly impressed the queen of Sheba (1 Ki. 10:5; 2 Chr. 9:4). Nehemiah was cupbearer to the Persian king Artaxerxes I Longimanus (Neh. 1:11), and he tells us that after he "took the wine and gave it to the king" (2:1), the two had a conversation involving new political action. The office of cupbearer was thus a highly influential one.

Dyer. The practice of dyeing textiles was in existence even before the time of Abraham. Vats and clay looms that were used as weights have been found in Lachish. Dyers obtained their dye from various sources. The crimson was obtained from a worm or grub that fed on the oak or other plants. Indigo was made from the rind of the pomegranate. Purple was made from the murex shellfish found on the beach at the city of Acre (Acco). It was also found along the Phoenician coast north of Acre. Luke tells of Lydia, "a dealer in purple cloth from the city of Thyatira" (Acts 16:14). Excavations have revealed that "a guild of dyers" existed in the vicinity of Thyatira.

Fishermen. The frequent allusions to the art of fishing in Scripture are in connection with the Sea of Galilee (Matt. 4:18; 13:48; Mk. 1:16; Lk. 5:2). Several methods of fishing were practiced. (a) The casting net was a common method used. The fisherman stood on the bank or waded breast-deep into the water and skillfully threw the net, which he had arranged on his arm, into the water in front of him. It fell in the shape of a ring, and as the weights dragged it down, the net took the shape of a dome or cone and enclosed the fish. (b) The dragnet was used in herring and salmon fishing, with floats marking the location of the submerged nets. It was usually operated from boats. (c) Hooks or angles were occasionally used. Fish were speared on the Mediterranean coast, being attracted to the surface by a moving torch. Night fishing was very common, especially on the Sea of Galilee.

Fuller. The skill of washing or bleaching clothes is one of the oldest arts. Both men and women engaged in cleaning clothes and other materials. The cleansing was done by treading or stamping the garments with the feet or with rods or sticks in containers of water. The fullers discovered a singular art of bleaching cloth white by the aid of alkali, soap, putrid urine, fumes of sulfur, and the ashes of certain desert plants. Therefore, the fuller's shop was located usually outside the city where offensive odors could be avoided; the cloth could be trampled clean in a running stream and then spread out for drying. In Jerusalem the "fuller's field" was located near the conduit of the upper pool, which was in all probability in the Kidron Valley between the Gihon Spring and the well En Rogel (2 Ki. 18:17; Isa. 7:3; 36:2).

Gatekeeper. The Levites who had charge of the various entrances to the temple were called gatekeepers or doorkeepers (1 Chr. 9:17; 15:18, 23–24; 2 Chr. 23:19). A gatekeeper was stationed at the city gates and among the shepherds, where he was responsible for guarding the doors of the sheepfold. In David's time, the gatekeepers of the temple, who were also guards, numbered four thousand (23:5).

Hunter. The work of hunter or fowler was one of the earliest occupations. It was originally a means of support, but it later became a source of recreation. It was held in very high repute and was engaged in by all classes, but more often by royalty (Gen. 10:9; 27:3, 5; 1 Sam. 26:20; Job 38:39; Prov. 6:5). Three principal methods of hunting are mentioned in the Bible: (a) shooting with bow and arrows (Exod. 27:3); (b) snaring by spring net and cage, especially for birds such as quail, partridge, and duck (Jer. 5:27; Amos 3:5); and (c) pits covered with a net and brushwood for deer, foxes, wolves, bears, lions, etc. (Ps. 35:7; Isa. 24:18; 42:22).

Judge. The head of the house was considered the judge over his own household. With the enlargement of the human family, this power quite naturally passed to the heads of tribes and clans. After Israel came into the wilderness beyond Sinai, Moses found the responsibility of handling all the judicial matters too great. Taking the advice of his father-in-law Jethro, he was advised to choose "men who fear God, trustworthy men who hate dishonest gain" to handle these matters. There were to be judges over thousands and hundreds and fifties (Exod. 18:19–26; Deut. 1:16). After coming into Canaan, judges sat at the gates of the cities (Deut. 16:18).

Lawyer. This term refers to one who is conversant with the law. There were court lawyers and synagogue lawyers (Matt. 22:35; Lk. 7:30; 10:25; 11:45–46, 52; 14:3; Tit. 3:13). The scribe functioned in the capacity of a lawyer in the pronouncement of legal decisions.

Merchant. People dealing in merchandise bought goods from distant lands or from caravans and sold them to traders in the marketplaces. Many became wealthy.

Sometimes merchants are spoken of appreciatively (2 Chr. 9:13–14; Cant. 3:6), but sometimes they were dishonest (Hos. 12:7), and, especially in the book of Revelation, they are condemned for seeking only material gain (Rev. 18:3, 11, 15, 23).

Musician. Since music was a very prominent art in biblical, especially OT, times and played such an important part in the life of Israel and in their religious exercises and festivities, there was a demand for those who were adept at playing instruments and in singing hymns and psalms (Ps. 68:25). Hebrew music was primarily vocal, yet many of the psalms have signs indicating that they were to be accompanied by musical instruments (1 Ki. 10:12; 2 Chr. 9:11; Rev. 18:12). The "chief musician" occurs in the titles of fifty-four psalms. Asaph and his brothers were apparently the first to hold this position, and the office was probably hereditary (1 Chr. 15:19; 2 Chr. 35:15). Among the instruments used by the Hebrews were the cymbal, harp, organ, pipe, psaltery, and trumpet. (See also chap. 4.)

Nurse. In ancient times the nurse had an honored position in a home, often as a nursemaid or nanny (2 Sam. 4:4; 2 Ki. 11:2). Most patriarchal families had a nurse or nurses. Rebekah's nurse went with her to Canaan and was buried with great mourning (Gen. 24:59; 35:8). Foster fathers or mothers were sometimes referred to as nurses (Ruth 4:16; Isa. 49:23).

Occultist. The Bible makes reference to (a) *diviners*, people who claimed to obtain secret knowledge, particularly of the future, and who stood in contrast to the prophets of the Lord (1 Sam. 6:2; Jer. 27:9; Zech. 10:2). (b) *Magicians* used superstitious ceremonies to hurt or to benefit others; they were sometimes able to duplicate the works of God (Gen. 41:8; Exod. 7:11, 22; Dan. 1:20; 2:2; 5:11; Acts 13:6, 8). (c) The *sorcerer* practiced the arts of the magicians and astrologers, by which he pretended to foretell events with the assistance of evil spirits (Isa. 47:9, 12; Acts 8:9, 11). (d) *Witches* or *mediums* were involved in apparent communication with demons and a pretended conversation with the spirits of the dead by means of which future events were revealed, diseases cured, and evil spirits driven away (Lev. 20:6; 1 Sam. 28; 2 Ki. 9:22).

Perfumer. All large oriental towns had their perfumers' street. Their stock included anything fragrant in the form of loose powder, compressed cake, or essences in spirit, oil, or fat, as well as seeds, leaves, and bark. Perfumes were used in connection with the holy oil and incense of the tabernacle (Exod. 30:25, 33, 35; 37:29; 2 Chr. 16:14; Neh. 3:8). The ritual of Baal-worshippers (Isa. 57:9) and the embalming of the dead and rites of burial (2 Chr. 16:14; Mk. 16:1; Lk. 23:56) all used perfume. The apothecary compounded and sold these sweet spices and anointing oils (Eccl. 10:1). The frequent references in the OT to physicians and perfumers indicate the high esteem in which the professions were held (Gen. 50:2; Jer. 8:22; Lk. 4:23).

Physician. This term refers to one who understands and practices medicine in the art of healing. The priests and prophets were expected to have some knowledge of medicine. In the days of Moses there were midwives and regular physicians who attended the Israelites (Exod. 1:19). They brought some knowledge of medicine with them from Egypt, whose physicians were renowned for their healing arts. The medicines prescribed were salves, particular balms, plaster and poultices, oil baths, mineral baths, etc. In Egypt the physicians also aided in carrying out the elaborate preparations connected with embalming a body (Gen. 50:2; see chap. 1).

Recorder. The recorder held an office of high rank in the Jewish state, exercising the functions not simply of an annalist, but also of chancellor or president of the privy council (Isa. 36:3, 22). He was not only the grand custodian of the public records, but he also kept the responsible registry of the current transactions of government (2 Sam. 8:16; 20:24; 2 Ki. 18:18). In David's court, the recorder appears among the high officers of his household (2 Sam. 8:16; 20:24). In Solomon's court, the recorder is associated with the three secretaries and is mentioned last, probably as being their president (1 Ki. 4:3).

Sailor. Because the Israelites never developed a maritime system, sailors are mentioned only in connection with foreign nations (1 Ki. 9:27; Jon. 1:5–7; cf. Rev. 18:17).

Scribe. Those who were employed to handle correspondence and to keep accounts were given a high place. See chap. 5 (section on Elders and Officials).

Soldier. In the days of Moses, every man above the age of twenty was a soldier (Num. 1:3); and each tribe formed a regiment, with its own banner and its own leader (2:2; 10:14). Up until the time of David, the army consisted entirely of infantry (1 Sam. 4:10; 15:4), the use of horses having been restrained by divine command (Deut. 17:16). See chap. 5 (sections on International Relations and Warfare).

Steward. Stewards were able men who were entrusted the management of the household (Gen. 43:19; Lk. 16:1).

Tanner. This term refers to someone who is skilled in dressing and preserving hides or skins of animals (Acts 9:43; 10:6, 32). Among the ancient Jews, ceremonial uncleanness was attached to the occupation of the tanner, and hence he was obliged to do his work outside the town.

Tax collector. The *publicans* (KJV) or tax collectors were hated for being the instruments through which the subjection of the Jews to the Roman emperor was perpetuated. They looked at the paying of tribute as a virtual acknowledgment of the emperor's sovereignty. Tax collectors were noted for imposing more taxes than were required so that they might more quickly enrich themselves. The publicans of the NT were regarded as traitors and apostates, defiled by their frequent contacts with pagans, and willing tools of the oppressor. Hence, they were classed with sinners, harlots, and pagans (Matt. 9:11; 21:31; Mk. 2:16; Lk. 5:27–30).

Teacher of the law. This title is often used synonymously with that of *scribe.* See chap. 6 (section on Scribes and Rabbis).

Woman weaving carpets.

Z. Radovan/www.BibleLandPictures.com

Looms are still used for interlacing yarns at right angles so as to form a cloth.

© Zondervan. Artist: Derrick McKenzie; Reconstruction/Archaeologist: Daniel Warner

Tentmaker. The early patriarchs largely lived in tents and were skilled in the art of tentmaking. In NT times it was the custom to teach every Jewish boy some trade. Jesus was a carpenter or builder, and Paul was a tentmaker. Paul practiced his trade in company with Aquila at Corinth (Acts 18:1–3).

Treasurer. Among the most important officials were those having charge of the receipts and disbursements of the public treasury (Ezra 1:8; 7:21; Isa. 22:15; Dan. 3:2–3). The title of treasurer was given to the officer of state, and the position was sometimes filled by the heir to the throne (2 Chr. 26:21).

Watchman. The need for security was met by having watchmen whose duty was to stand in the tower on the walls or at the gates of the city. They also patrolled the streets, and, besides protecting the city and its inhabitants from violence, they were required to call out the hours of the night (2 Sam. 18:24–27; Cant. 5:7; Isa. 21:11–12).

Weaver. There was constant need of those skilled in the making of cloth or rugs from spun thread or string. The Israelites probably perfected the art of weaving while in Egypt, though they no doubt made progress in it from their own resources, even before they entered Egypt. Weaving, for the most part, was done by women. The fibrous materials woven were usually linen, flax, and wool (Exod. 35:35; Lev. 13:48; 1 Chr. 11:23; Isa. 38:12).

Commerce and Economics

The items produced by work were not only consumed or used locally, but also exchanged among different sections of Palestine and beyond. The shepherds and farmers exchanged produce and sheep. The maker of charcoal found a market in areas where the forests had been cut down. The coastal cities and Jericho sold salt to the inland population. Carpenters were probably often paid in kind by the people for whom they worked.

Palestine had a few major exports for nearby nations. Because the Phoenicians needed food, central and northern Palestine sold to them grains and olive oil, wine and food animals. Egypt had plenty of grain and animals, but she needed olive oil and wine. When the camel made trade with Arabia common, the caravans sought Palestinian food stuffs. Raisins, dried figs, and dates were probably international produce because they were easily transported. Linen was sold to all nearby nations except Egypt, which made the best linen.

Natural products other than those already mentioned were primarily copper, bitumen, and raw wool. Since iron was the ideal metal in Solomon's day and quite inexpensive (Gilead was a major center for iron ore), he sold his copper to the backward people in the Red Sea area. In return Solomon received gold, precious incense, and rare spices.

Bitumen had a good market in Egypt, Palestine, and the adjacent lands. Its source was the Dead Sea; its quality was excellent, but the quantity was small, quite the opposite of Mesopotamia. Sulphur was also a natural product from the Dead Sea area.

Palestine always produced more wool than she could manufacture, so this was a constant export commodity, especially to heavily populated areas. Moab was the major wool producer. Palestine also exported rare resins and gums, such as myrrh and balm. The latter was very expensive and was a major source of income for Herod the Great, from his vast balm groves at Jericho.

Industry's greatest change came in the cloth market. Kiriath Sepher (or Debir, some eight miles southwest of Hebron), when excavated, turned out to be a one-industry town. It was located in a fine sheep district, and the whole city was given over to the weaving and dyeing of cloth. Every house had large looms and dye plants, each one of them standardized. The raw material was right at the "factory's" door, and both industries had a heavy and constant market. Most manufactured goods were sold in Palestine itself and did not reach international markets.

Palestine's major commercial neighbor on the south was Egypt, one of the great civilizations of antiquity. It is no surprise to discover the strong influence of Egyptian commerce in the objects found in the excavations in Palestine. Even Ethiopia sent ebony to Palestine, and part of the ivory

Remains of a Roman road on the Ascent of Adumim, near Jericho.

Todd Bolen/www.BiblePlaces.com

probably came via the Sudan. The main trade road left Egypt about where the modern Suez Canal is located and then followed along the coast past Raphia, ending at Gaza.

Palestine's commercial neighbor on the southeast was Arabia. Her water commerce came to Ezion Geber on the Gulf of Aqabah and then it was carried by camel caravan north to Macan. This Arabian commerce consisted entirely of luxury items, such as gold, frankincense, myrrh, coral, pearls, emeralds, agates, and other precious stones. Rare spices and scented woods of various kinds from India also came in via Arabia.

To the northeast of Palestine was Syria. Although these two countries produced similar products, they did have some commercial dealings. Damascus was rightly called the "seaport for all the desert people." The important fact is that the route by which both Mesopotamian and Anatolian commerce went south to Egypt was via Syria and Palestine. Anatolia (Asia Minor) was one of the world's most important sources of metals in antiquity. There the Hittites and their successors were the miners, smelters, and refiners of copper, silver, and iron ores. They also manufactured all types of metal wares.

Just north of Palestine and bordering the Mediterranean was Phoenicia. Like England at her peak, it was both a manufacturing and maritime nation. This was the country that taught Greece to become a manufacturer. Phoenicia's major natural resource was her cedar forests, whose lumber all the world prized. Her wares ran from excellent to mediocre. The most important international product she manufactured was purple dyed cloth. The wool was imported, but the cloth and dye were Phoenician.

During the period between the Old and New Testaments, Alexander's successors revolutionized some of the Palestinian business. Greek became the dominant influence. All over the world people of many nationalities suddenly became Hellenized. There is not too much information from this period concerning trade and commerce in Palestine. One major improvement was the quality of flax, which, woven into first-class linen, went into the international market. The fisheries around the Sea of Galilee prospered, exporting their salted fish as far as Rome.

When the Mediterranean became Roman property, sea commerce took on new life. The major harbors were expanded to handle the increased commerce. Rome was fed in large part from the grain of North Africa and of the valleys of the Nile in Egypt and the Orontes in Syria.

As a result of the Diaspora (Dispersion), the Jew was a world citizen and was often involved in world trade (Acts 2:9–11 mentions the many countries settled by Jewish people). Antioch of Syria was the second most influential city in the world, although Alexandria outranked it in size. Antioch was the end of the road for all overland commerce coming in from China via Persia to the Mediterranean. Alexandria, on the other hand, was the shipping point for all African commerce, whether it came via the Nile River or the Red Sea. There were no major seaports between these two cities but a wealth of local ports, some of which Paul used. Antioch catered primarily to the luxury trade, and the world was as avid for luxuries then as now. Alexandria catered to both the common and luxury markets.

When money becomes a major factor in trade and commerce, the emphasis is on business, for the common denominator in all business is money. In the OT there were three major methods of sale: (a) barter,

(b) weighing of silver or gold, and later (c) coins. Barter was the most common method of sale among the poorer people, although even King Solomon and King Hiram used the method: Hiram furnished cedar and cypress wood to Solomon, who, in turn, gave wheat and olive oil to Hiram (1 Ki. 5:10–11). These farm products were the taxes Solomon had collected, for taxes were at that time paid in kind.

If commerce is to be successful in international markets it must have a basic medium of exchange, for which the ancients used silver and/or gold. The former was rarer and thus more valuable until the metallurgists solved the problem of smelting and refining complicated silver ores. Gold, then, took first place. These metals came in various sized rings, bars, and other shapes. The Hebrew term for "silver" (*keseph*) was equivalent to "money" (e.g., Isa. 55:1). If a less valuable metal was used as money, it was copper. Rare gems and expensive jewelry also served as money. They provided the means whereby a large amount of wealth could be transported easily and secretly.

The metals were weighed, and this act often turned dishonest. Archaeologists have found weights with which to purchase items and a different set of weights by which to sell that same purchase. This dishonesty is referred to in Deut. 25:13, "Do not have two differing weights in your bag—one heavy, one light." In Amos 8:5, the prophet echoes the same theme and adds that dry measures were used dishonestly in his day (cf. Deut. 25:14).

The next step in currency was the coin. Not only was there dishonesty in the weight of gold and silver bars, etc., but there was a wide variety in the purity of the metal, especially in silver. That problem was solved by governments minting coins and guaranteeing the weight and purity of each coin struck. This was done by putting the symbol of that government (state or city) upon the coin. The first such coin mentioned in the Bible is the Persian gold daric (Ezra 2:69). The Persians permitted the Jewish exiles to mint their own silver coins in Judea. Coins did not become commonplace in Palestine until the times of the Ptolemies and the Seleucids.

In NT times a denarius was the laborer's standard wage for one day's work.

Jay King

Where money is used—either the weighing of gold or silver, or the use of the coin—the banker is present, and money itself becomes a new commodity. There is no evidence of OT banking, but early Mesopotamia was very efficient in banking methods. During the exile, the Jews learned Babylonian banking techniques. Jewish bankers from Babylon were widely used later by the successors of Alexander the Great. The exile marked the beginning of the Jews' major emphasis on banking and business in general. This was augmented by Jewish business exiles in the intertestamental times who were taken to Alexandria, where they later controlled

Treasury of the Athenians at Delphi, Greece.

much of the business of that city. This meant branch offices for the Jewish enterprises in all the seaports of the Roman empire.

By NT times, banking covered the whole Roman empire, and bankers were licensed to be kept under control. The banker, then as now, took money on deposit and paid interest for its use. Jesus referred to this practice in his parable of the talents (Matt. 25:27). A common interest rate was 8 percent in the days of Jesus and Paul. The banker then, as now, lent this money on mortgages. The earliest Bible reference to a mortgage is Neh. 5:3. The people borrowed money to pay their taxes (vv. 4–5), just as people do today. One position of the banking fraternity was the money changer (Jn. 2:14–16).

Checks were used then as now, and bills of exchange were available, that is, one could deposit money in one city and draw it out in another. Banks related to one another were scattered all over the empire. Good bookkeeping systems, however, were much earlier than banking; they can be traced to the early Sumerians, who invented writing.

Chapter 4

Society

Individuals relate to one another not only in a family setting and in connection with their work, but also in the broader society of which they are a part. This chapter discusses various aspects of life in Israelite society.

Societal Relations

The biblical emphasis on the parent-child relationship (e.g., Exod. 20:12) makes clear that the home was viewed as the primary unit of society. Moreover, the solidarity of familial (or clan) life is reflected in a number of customs, such as the institution of levirate marriage (Deut. 25:5–6; Lk. 20:28; see chap. 1). At the same time, the "assembly of the LORD" (cf. the use of the term in Deut. 23:1–3, 8) was regarded as possessing a unity of its own, so that exclusion from it amounted to virtual exile.

During OT times, the individual enjoyed a real but limited role as a unit within society. Gifted individuals, including some women, rose to positions of recognized leadership, outstandingly during the time of the judges. Property rights were protected in basic law (Exod. 20:15), so that unlawful alienation of property was punished and restitution carefully specified. Damage to life and limb was controlled early by the principle of equivalence ("an eye for an eye"), but it seems clear that this code, along with the ancient practice of blood-revenge, was modified by the imposition of an alternate material restitution. Punishment for unintentional maiming and manslaughter was controlled by the institution of cities of refuge.

While there was no overt distinction between public and private morality, it is clear that the ancient Hebrews, guided by divine inspiration, sought to apply principles to both interpersonal and interracial relationships reflective of their high providential origin as a people. There was a progressive elimination of purely tribal customs, a reduction of the number of capital crimes, and a concern for "widow, orphan, and stranger" that marked off Israel's societal life qualitatively from other social patterns of the times. Interracial relationships often were corrupted by the brutalities of invading peoples, and Israel's practices frequently reflected all too clearly the social evils of her environing nations. At the same time, Israel made a good showing in overall societal relationship when compared with other peoples of the ancient world.

In other respects, the relation of the individual to society varied from one epoch of Israel's history to another. With the development of the national self-consciousness within Israel—which rested on the covenant of Abraham and the events surrounding the exodus from Egypt and the giving of the law at Sinai—there emerged a tendency toward separateness, not only with respect to environing nations, but also at the point of interpersonal relations between Hebrews and non-Hebrews. On the other hand, there was a certain cosmopolitanism within the Levitical legislation, so that Israel's experiences in Egypt were to be regarded as a reminder that the people's treatment of the "stranger" was to be humane and even cordial (cf. Exod. 23:9; Deut. 24:20).

On the whole, it may be said that prior to the Babylonian exile societal relations between Israel and neighboring people as persons was moderately cordial, so that, for instance, Uriah the Hittite was a trusted officer under David (2 Sam. 11:6–17), Ittai the Gittite was captain of David's personal guard (18:2), the Kenites were treated as relatives (Jdg. 1:16; 5:24), and strangers in general had the right of asylum in Israel's cities of refuge (Num. 35:15).

Conditions deteriorated with the return of the exiles from the captivity. No doubt the ruthless treatment of Jews during the exile afforded a background for the growing antipathy of postexilic Jewish society for the Gentiles. Contributive to this polarity was also the strict reform that separated many mixed marriages under Ezra (Ezra 10:18–44). As necessary as these reform measures may have been, they could not have failed to generate much tension between Jews and the peoples from whom the foreign wives came.

Tensions during the intertestamental period were aggravated by the hardening of the divisions between the Jewish people and the Samaritans and even more by the efforts of Antiochus IV in the second century BC to humiliate and to Hellenize the Jews. Thus by NT times we read, for example, that "Jews do not associate with Samaritans" (Jn. 4:9). And the loss of political freedom in 63 BC, when the Romans occupied Jerusalem, greatly intensified the rift between Jew and Gentile.

Population

Estimating the size of the Israelite population in OT times is a challenge. The difficulties begin when we read that the fighting force of the Israelites in the wilderness consisted of some 600,000 men (Num. 1:46; 26:51), which means that the nation as a whole must have numbered at least two million people and maybe as many as five million. Such figures seem out of kilter with other data available to us. For example, the armies of such great empires as Egypt and Assyria usually numbered only in the tens of thousands, so an Israelite army in the hundreds of thousands would have completely overwhelmed the Canaanites and made it impossible for them to resist (archaeological investigation indicates that the total population of Canaan at this time was less than three million). Indeed, why would Joshua have taken only thirty thousand men (Josh. 8:3) to fight against Ai, where they suffered a great defeat, if more than half a million were available?

Some have thought that the large numbers in the biblical record had some kind of symbolism now lost to us. Others argue that the Hebrew word for "thousand" here refers to a military unit or "troop," so that the Israelite army consisted of six hundred troops, with a total of perhaps thirty to sixty thousand soldiers. These and other suggestions are problematic as well, however, and a final solution has not been reached.

In any case, there is other information that allows us to form a general picture of the Israelite population after the conquest of Canaan. We know, for example, that the vast majority of settlements and villages would have consisted of only a few hundred people, with a small proportion of towns having populations of a thousand or more.

Very few cities would have had inhabitants in the tens of thousands.

The growth of Jerusalem (earlier called Jebus, Jdg. 19:10) serves to illustrate the situation. When David conquered the city (2 Sam. 5:6–7), it occupied only the southeastern hill, covering no more than fifteen acres. A reasonable estimate is that at this time Jerusalem had about three thousand inhabitants. During the reigns of David and Solomon, the city no doubt expanded, and some time later it included the southwestern hill. When the Assyrians conquered the northern tribes, many Israelites would have escaped to the south, settling in Jerusalem and its environs. Recent evidence makes clear that by the time of Hezekiah the city covered well over one hundred acres, with a population of over twenty thousand. Jerusalem was destroyed in 586 BC, then resettled within a century. By NT times, the city had perhaps around fifty thousand permanent inhabitants, although the population swelled at the time of Passover and other feasts.

As for the entire nation, archaeological evidence suggests that soon after the death of Solomon the total may have been around one million and that the northern kingdom of Israel may have had twice as many inhabitants as the southern kingdom of Judah. The centuries that followed saw growth, then decline at the time of the Assyrian and Babylonian invasions, then growth again, especially after the Romans conquered Palestine. For example, Lower Galilee, which lay across the commercial axes of the land and was favored both by climate and by situation, grew significantly. It is estimated that around the middle of the first century AD its population was possibly 400,000 and that it possessed at least nine towns with more than 15,000 inhabitants each.

The Jordan River Valley.

More significant than the size of the population was its character. As already mentioned, foreigners were sometimes integrated into Israelite society, though it is difficult to assess how substantial their numbers were. Beyond that, the population was undoubtedly stratified. As in most societies, for example, the nobility played an important role (see chap. 5).

There has been much discussion regarding the Hebrew term *Am ha-arez* (or *Am ha-arets*), which means "the people of the land." Although the phrase can be used in a general sense, such as "natives" or "inhabitants" (cf. Gen. 23:7; 42:6; Num. 13:28), it usually seems to refer more strictly to the responsible male citizenry who lived on their own land, served in the army, and participated in judicial proceedings and cult festivals. They may have had a leading role in the achievement of partial reform under Joash (2 Ki. 11:13–18) and fuller restoration under Josiah (21:24). As the hard core of Israel, these people who owned and defended the land were also the special target of foreign powers who levied indemnities and taxes (23:35; 25:18–21). After OT times, however, *Am ha-arez* became a term of contempt for common people who were not meticulous about keeping the law (cf. Jn. 7:49). This use, as preserved in the rabbinic literature, almost completely overshadowed the earlier connotation.

Slavery

The number of slaves in Israel probably did not run as high as in classical times, since it would have been cheaper to hire laborers for work. The use of slaves seems to have been

Assyrian relief from Sennacherib's palace (Nineveh, c. 700 BC) showing slaves or prisoners at work on building projects.

Z. Radovan/www.BibleLandPictures.com

largely confined to household duties and to work in the field alongside the master and his family.

The earliest means for the acquisition of slaves in the ancient Near East was by military conquest. Thousands of men, women, and children were thus reduced to servitude. To the ancients this was considered a humanitarian improvement on the earlier practice of killing all of the enemy. Various legal codes, including those in OT law, sought to limit the excesses of brutal punishment that captives received. The Hebrew, for example, was told that if a soldier saw a beautiful woman among the captives and married her, he must treat her thereafter as a free person; moreover, he was not permitted to sell her into slavery if he ceased to delight in her (Deut. 21:10–14).

The OT provided that foreigners could be bought and sold as slaves and considered as property (Lev. 25:44–46). There are infrequent references to foreign slaves who were imported into Palestine (1 Chr. 2:34–35). Hebrews were also sold into slavery in other lands; hence the death penalty was prescribed for those who kidnapped and sold a freeborn person (Exod. 21:16; Deut. 24:7). The OT cites examples of a father selling his daughter (Exod. 21:7; Neh. 5:5); a widow selling her children to pay her husband's debt (2 Ki. 4:1); and men and women selling themselves (Lev. 25:39, 47; Deut. 15:12–17).

The price of slaves varied widely. Thirty shekels was the price according to Exod. 21:32. A scale of from three to fifty shekels is given in Lev. 27:3–7, according to the age and sex of the slave. An appeal could be made to a priest when there was disagreement on price (v. 8). Twenty shekels was the price for a young man (v. 5)—the price paid for Joseph (Gen. 37:28). In intertestamental times the average price for a slave was forty shekels (2 Macc. 8:11). A ransom of one talent for a captive (1 Ki. 20:39) must indicate that he was an individual of great importance.

Children were sold into slavery under terms of a conditional contract. More frequently this was true of young, unmarried girls. Exodus 21 stipulates that if a man sells his daughter, she must become the wife or concubine of her master or of one of his sons when she reaches maturity. If no male member of the family takes her as a wife, she is to be set free without any payment of money from her (v. 11). This condition was put in the contract because young girls were frequently purchased with the intention of making prostitutes of them when they reached maturity. A forced sale of children into slavery is mentioned in Neh. 5:1–5. Presumably a father had pledged his children for loans during a time of economic hardship. As settlement for the debts the land was seized and the children were sold into slavery.

There is some evidence that the Hebrews did traffic in slaves. An Egyptian slave is mentioned in 1 Chr. 2:34. Two laws dealt with slave trade. Both Exod. 21:16 and Deut. 24:7 forbid the kidnapping and selling of freeborn individuals; the penalty for such was death. It is quite possible that some were being sold into foreign countries. In earlier times, Joseph certainly was handled in this fashion (Gen. 37:28). A second law (Deut. 23:15–16) prohibits the extradition of a runaway slave, presumably a Hebrew who had escaped from his master in a foreign country.

Self-sale into slavery seems to have been a common practice of the Israelites. The Mosaic law included a provision regarding the person who refused to go free after some years of service (Exod. 21:5–6; Deut.

15:16–17). If he refused his freedom because he enjoyed the economic security of his new home, and because he wished to remain with the wife his master provided for him, and with his children, he would serve his master for life. Leviticus 25 describes the way in which an Israelite was to be treated who entered into the state of slavery voluntarily or who sold himself to a fellow Israelite or resident foreigner.

One of the chief sources of slaves in Palestine consisted of citizens who were in default of payment for their debts (Exod. 21:2–4; Deut. 15:12). A number of those who joined David at the cave of Adullam were defaulting debtors (1 Sam. 22:2). Other passages mention instances of children who were seized to satisfy creditors (2 Ki. 4:1; Neh. 5:1–5; cf. Isa. 50:1).

The OT law regarding the release of slaves is stated in three passages (Exod. 21:1–11; Lev. 25:39–55; Deut. 15:12–18). The first of these provided that a male Hebrew slave should be freed after he had served six years. If he was married before he became a slave, his wife was to be released with him; if he was provided a wife by his master, the slave could go free, but his wife and children would remain the property of the owner. In such instances, if the slave chose to remain with his master and his wife and children, he was to appear before the judges, have his ear pierced, presumably for some tag to be affixed, and become a slave for life.

The law of release found in Lev. 25:39–55 provided that a Hebrew could never be in perpetual bondage. An Israelite who sold himself into slavery was to be released in the Jubilee Year. He was not to be considered a slave, but a bondservant or hireling. True slaves were acquired from the surrounding nations, and for them there was no release. They were inherited with other property (vv. 44–46). A third provision required that if a Hebrew sold himself because of poverty to a resident foreigner, one of his relatives would have the right to redeem him. The price was to be based on the amount for which he was originally acquired, prorated to the number of years left to Jubilee. He was to be released in the year of Jubilee if not redeemed before then.

The slave was considered to be a part of his owner's family; hence he shared in their religious life. The laws guaranteed him a right to the Sabbath rest (Exod. 20:10; 23:12) and granted him a share in the religious feasts (Deut. 12:12; 16:11, 14). Thus the sojourner could not partake of the feast until he had been circumcised, but the slave, who as a member of the family had to be circumcised, always took part in the feasts (Exod. 12:43–45). Likewise, a slave in the house of a priest was allowed to eat of the offering of the holy things, but a sojourner in the household, or even the daughter of a priest if she had married into a non-priestly family, was forbidden to share in the offering (Lev. 22:10–12).

Slaves were protected in considerable measure from inhumane treatment. The murder of a slave was punishable by death (Exod. 21:12). If a master beat a slave, and he died as a result, the master was to be punished, but it is not clear what the punishment was (21:20–21). Again, if a master maimed his slave, the slave was to be set free (21:26). The terms of the prohibition on maiming were quite restrictive. A slave was to be set free if a beating resulted even in the loss of a tooth (21:27). Restrictions were also placed on the illegal sale of persons into slavery and on the return of runaway slaves.

From earliest times slaves were granted the right to accumulate almost any form of personal property, including their own slaves (2 Sam. 9:10). According to Lev. 25:47–55, a man who sold himself into slavery might be redeemed by his nearest kin or by his own acquired wealth ("if he prospers, he may redeem himself," v. 49). A unique provision for Hebrew slaves is to be found in Deut. 15:13–15: a slave who was freed in the sabbatical year was to be provided with goods from the increase of his master's prosperity as a reminder to all that the Hebrews were delivered from bondage in Egypt.

State slavery existed from earliest recorded time in the ancient Near East. First mention of it in Israel is made in Josh. 16:10 and Jdg. 1:28 in reference to work performed for the state by the Canaanites after the conquest of the land. State slavery evidently became more widespread and more important economically when the Davidic kingdom was established. Under Solomon, slaves in large numbers were used by the state to work copper mines and mills. Because of extremely harsh working conditions, they must have died in great numbers. Perhaps it was for this purpose that Solomon reduced to slavery all the descendants of "the Amorites, Hittites, Perizzites, Hivites and Jebusites" that the Israelites had not been able to exterminate (1 Ki. 9:20–21).

Temple slaves or servants ("Nethinim") were common in OT times, although no mention of them was made until postexilic times. They were brought back by Zerubbabel and Ezra from Babylonia (Ezra 2:43–54; Neh. 7:46–56). Ezra states that there were 220 of them whom David and his officials had set apart to attend the Levites (Ezra 8:20). They apparently lived in separate quarters adjoining the temple and worked under supervisors (Neh. 3:31; 11:21). Earlier in biblical history, mention is made of captives who served in the tabernacle: these included Midianites given to the priests and Levites before the Israelites entered the Promised Land (Num. 31:25–40).

The legal codes tell little of what it was like to be a slave. For that, one can only turn to OT narratives in which slaves were important figures. It should be noted first that slaves were members of the household and were grouped with the women and children (Exod. 20:17). The latter, like slaves, could be bought and sold. The wife and the slave-concubine were often hard to distinguish.

Generally slaves were not owned in large numbers in Palestine except by the temple and the state. Slaves were usually domestics in the households of the well-to-do rather than agricultural or handicraft workers in large-scale operations. A warm affection frequently developed between master and slave. The codes in both Exodus and Deuteronomy specifically made provision for the slave who wished to remain in bondage because of his affection for his master. Such a relationship must have existed earlier between Abraham and Eliezer of Damascus, for this servant was at one time designated the heir of his master (Gen. 15:1–4), and later he was sent to negotiate a marriage for the heir (chap. 24). A slave of Saul was an adviser and confidant of his master (1 Sam. 9:5; 16:22), as was Gehazi, the slave of Elisha (2 Ki. 4:12; 8:4). Mention is also made of one Jarha, an Egyptian slave in the household who was given the daughter of his master in marriage (1 Chr. 2:35). Thus the frequent picture that is drawn is one of affection and trust on the part of both master and slave, very much within the confines of the family.

Slavery had a long history in the Greco-Roman world prior to NT times. Most slaves were inherited or purchased. The latter were usually prisoners of war or persons illegally seized and sold by pirates to slave traders. Some few slave traders seem to have engaged in the ugly trade of breeding and selling slaves, a common business in earlier centuries. Indebtedness was a cause of slavery in early Rome, but this practice was forbidden by law long before the NT period.

During the third to first centuries BC, slaves were introduced into Roman society by the hundreds of thousands. However, one must be careful not to assign the barbaric treatment of slaves by the Romans in the pre-Christian centuries to the early Christian era. Sweeping humanitarian changes had been introduced into the Roman world by the first century AD, and these led to radically improved treatment of slaves, who had most of the legal rights that were granted to the freeborn. Many had a considerable amount of money at their disposal and had rights to wife and family. In AD 20 a decree of the senate specified that slave criminals were to be tried in the same way as free men.

The living conditions of many slaves were better than those of free men, who often slept in the streets of the city or lived in very cheap rooms. Moreover, the slave was not inferior to the free person of similar skills in regard to food and clothing. The average free laborer at Rome and in the provinces could expect to earn about one denarius a day (cf. Matt. 20:2), and this amount was barely enough to meet basic necessities. Slaves, in addition to having their basic expenses provided for, received a modest amount as spending money. And in time of economic hardship, it was the slave and not the free man who was guaranteed the necessities of life for himself and his family.

It was not uncommon for a slave to become a citizen. Indeed, evidence of various kinds indicates that the Romans freed slaves in great numbers. Under the name and patronage of a former master, the freedman could fulfill obligations to the state, the most important of which was military service. The master frequently established his freedman in a business, and the master became a shareholder in it. Usually the slave had learned his trade as an apprentice in the master's household or handicraft shop. By extra labor slaves could save enough to buy their freedom, or it was granted gratuitously by their masters. Once freed, they often became prosperous.

Dress

Our knowledge of the kind of clothing worn by the people of biblical times comes from statements in both the OT and the NT, but also from burial remains and from representations of the people and their clothing found on monuments, reliefs, seals, plaques, and tomb paintings. All these, coupled with the traditions and usages extant among the present bedouin Arab tribes, lead us to conclude that at a very early period people learned the art of spinning and weaving cloth of hair, wool, cotton, flax, and eventually silk (Gen. 14:23; 31:18–19; 37:3; 38:28; Job 7:6; Ezek. 16:10, 13).

The clothing worn by the Hebrew people of biblical times was graceful, modest, and exceedingly significant. It was considered so much a part of those who wore it that it told who and what they were; moreover, it was intended as an external symbol of the individual's innermost feelings and deepest desires and his or her moral urge to represent God aright. With certain kinds of cloth and with astonishingly vivid colors of white, purple, scarlet, blue, yellow, and black, it represented the state of their minds and emotions. When joyful and ready to enter into festive occasions, they donned their clothing of brightest array; and when they mourned or humbled themselves, they put on sackcloth—literally cloth from which sacks were made—which was considered the very poorest kind of dress and quite indicative of their lowly feelings (1 Ki. 20:31–32; Job 16:15; Isa. 15:3; Jer. 4:8; 6:26; Lam. 2:10; Ezek. 7:18; Dan. 9:3; Joel 1:8).

There was variety in clothing characterizing the people from the various lands adjacent to Palestine, and within the narrow confines of the country itself there was a distinctive clothing that set off the Canaanite from the Philistine. Among the Hebrews there were slight differences in dress characterizing rank, trade, and profession. Yet it was little less than amazing how similar the general patterns were. The variety for the most part was in quality and in decoration. Clothing was colored—red, brown, yellow, etc—but white was much preferred. It denoted purity, cleanliness, and joy. Princes, priests, and kings wore purple, except on special occasions when they often dressed in white garments. Others sometimes wore white on the occasions of joy and gladness. But in general the people wore darker colors.

The basic garments used by men in biblical times seem to have consisted of the *inner-tunic*, the *tunic-coat*, the *girdle*, and the *cloak*. Added to this was the *headdress* and the *shoes* or *sandals*.

The inner-tunic or undershirt was usually made of a long piece of plain cotton or linen cloth made into a short shirt-like undergarment. At times it was little more than a loincloth in length, and at other times it reached below the knees or even just above the ankles. It was not usually worn when the weather was warm.

The tunic-coat, a close-fitting shirt-like garment, was the piece of clothing most frequently worn in the home and on the street. In ancient times it was often of one solid color, but at the present it is more often made of a brightly colored striped cotton material that among the Arabs is often called "the cloth of seven colors" because of the narrow vertical stripes of green, red, yellow, blue, and white that alternate. It was lined with a white cotton material and worn over the undershirt when the weather was cool, but next to the body when it was warm. This garment usually had long sleeves and extended down to the ankles when worn as a dress coat and was held in place by a girdle. Hard-working men, slaves, and prisoners wore them more abbreviated—sometimes even to their knees and without sleeves.

The girdle was a belt made of either cloth or leather, which was worn over the loose coat-like skirt or shirt. The cloth girdle, ordinarily worn by village and townspeople, was a square yard of woolen, linen, or even silk cloth first made into a triangle, then folded into a sash-like belt about six inches wide and some thirty-six inches long. When drawn about the waist and the tapering ends tied in the back, it not only formed a belt, but its folds formed a pocket to carry a variety of articles such as nuts, loose change, and other small objects or treasures. It was worn by both men and women, and the model woman of Prov. 31 made them to sell to the merchants. The girdle is not only a picturesque article of dress but also may indicate the position and office of the wearer. It is sometimes used to signify power and strength (2 Sam. 22:40; Isa. 11:5; Jer. 13:1; Eph. 6:14).

The leather girdle or belt was about four inches wide and was often studded with iron, silver, or gold. It was worn by soldiers, by men of the desert, and by countrymen who tended cattle or engaged in the rougher pursuits of life. This type of girdle was

The attire of Israelite nobles is depicted in this relief from Shalmaneser III's Black Obelisk.

Z. Radovan/www.BibleLandPictures.com

sometimes supported by a shoulder strap and provided a means whereby various articles such as a scrip (a small bag or wallet for carrying small articles), sword, dagger, or other valuables could be carried. It was the kind of girdle worn by Elijah (2 Ki. 1:8) and by John the Baptist (Matt. 3:4). Today the laborer and the poorer classes use rawhide or rope for a girdle; the better classes use woolen or camel's hair sashes of different widths.

The girdle, whether made of cloth or leather, was a very useful article of clothing and often entered into many activities of everyday life. When one was to walk or run or begin any type of service he "girded himself" for the journey or for the task at hand. Girded loins became a symbol of readiness for service or endeavor (cf. Isa. 11:5; Eph. 6:14).

The cloak (or mantle or robe) was a large, loose-fitting garment, which for warmth and appearance was worn over all other articles of clothing as a completion of male attire. It was distinguished by its greater size and by the absence of the girdle. It existed in two varieties. One of them, the *me'il*, was a long, loose-sleeved robe or public dress worn chiefly by men of official position and by ministers, educators, and the wealthy; it was the mark of high rank and station (1 Sam. 24:11; 1 Chr. 15:27). In its finest form, it must have been the high priest's robe of the ephod with its fringe of bells and pomegranates swaying and swinging and tinkling as he walked (Exod. 28:31–38). The *simlah* was a large sleeveless cloak that, in general pattern, corresponds to the long and flowing garment that the Arab shepherd and peasant call an *abba* or *abayeh*. They wear it by day and wrap themselves in it by night. Understandably, it was not to be taken in pledge unless it was returned by sundown (Exod. 22:26–27).

Both of these simple yet picturesque garments were usually made of wool, goat hair, or camel hair. Men of distinction often wore more colorful cloaks made of linen, wool, velvet, or silk, elaborately bordered and lined with fur. This long outer garment or topcoat was, in all probability, the "mantle" worn by Elijah and Elisha (2 Ki. 2:8–14 KJV). It was the camel-hair garment worn by John the Baptist (Matt. 3:4). It is frequently made of alternate strips of white, red, and brown or is formed by sewing together two lengths of cloth so that the only seams required were those along the top of the shoulders. In unusual cases, however, the cloak is woven of one broad width, with no seam. Many believe that this was the garment Christ wore and over which, at the crucifixion, the Roman soldiers "cast lots" rather than tearing it, for it was "seamless, woven in one piece from top to bottom" (Jn. 19:23–24).

The headdress was worn chiefly as a protection against the sun and as a finish to a completed costume. It varied from time to time according to rank, sex, and nationality. In the main, however, there were three known types that were worn by the male members of the Hebrew and surrounding nations. (a) The ordinary brimless cotton or woolen *cap*, corresponding somewhat to our skullcap, was sometimes worn by men of poorer circumstances. (b) The *turbans* were made of thick linen material and formed by winding a scarf or sash about the head in artistic style and neatly concealing the ends. The high priest wore a turban of fine linen (Exod. 28:39; KJV, "mitre"). (c) The *headscarf*, known among the Arabs as the *kaffiyeh*, is usually made up of a square yard of white or colored cotton, wool, or silk cloth folded into a triangle and draped about the head. The apex of the triangle falls directly down the back, forming a V point, while the tapering ends are thrown back over the shoulders, or in cold weather they are wrapped about the neck.

Shoes and sandals were considered the lowliest articles that went to make up the wearing apparel of the people of Bible lands (Mk. 1:7). Shoes were of soft leather, while sandals were of a harder leather and were worn for rougher wear. According to some authorities, the sole was of wood, cane, or sometimes bark of the palm tree, and it was fastened to the leather by nails. They were tied about the feet with a "thong" (Gen. 14:23; KJV, "shoelatchet"). It was customary to have two pairs, especially on a journey. Shoes were usually removed at the doorway before entering a home, on approaching God (Exod. 3:5), and during mourning (2 Sam. 15:30).

A few articles of female clothing carried somewhat the same name and basic pattern, yet there was always sufficient difference in embossing, embroidery, and needlework so that in appearance the line of demarcation between men and women could be readily detected. The women wore long garments reaching almost to the feet, with a girdle of silk or wool, many times having all the colors of the rainbow. Often such a garment

An Egyptian child's sandals (15th cent. BC).

Z. Radovan/www.BibleLandPictures.com

would have a fringe hanging from the waist nearly to the ankles.

The ladies' headdress usually included some kind of a *kaffiyeh* or cloth for covering the head, yet the material that was in that covering was of different quality, kind, or color from that worn by the men. Also, it was often pinned over some kind of a cap made of stiff material and set with pearls, silver, gold, or spangled ornaments common to that day. A woman would probably wear a long gown with long, pointed sleeves. Over this was a small rather tightly fitted jacket made of "scarlet" or other good material and was a thing of exquisite beauty because it was covered with "tapestry" or fine needlework, wrought with multicolored threads. A woman of even moderate circumstances could have beautiful clothing, for it was "the fruit of her own hands."

Women often added to their adornment by an elaborate braiding of the hair. Peter found it necessary to warn Christian women against relying on such adorning to make themselves attractive (1 Pet. 3:3). Earrings and nose-rings were especially common. Rings were worn by both men and women. All ancient Israelites wore signet rings or seals (Gen. 38:18). Rings were often worn on the toes, anklets (spangles) on the ankles (Isa. 3:18), and bracelets on the arms and wrists (Gen. 24:22; Ezek. 16:11).

The style of women's dress in the Middle East has not changed significantly over the centuries.

Library of Congress, LC-DIG-matpc-06018

Beginning about the second century BC, all male Jews were expected to wear at morning prayers, except on Sabbaths and festivals, two *phylacteries*, one on the forehead, called a *frontlet*, the other on the left arm. They consisted of small leather cases containing four passages of Scripture from the OT (Exod. 13:1–10, 11–16; Deut. 6:4–9; 11:13–21).

Music

The cultural life of Israel was intimately bound with the nation's religion, a subject to be treated later (see chap. 6). This feature is especially obvious with regard to literature. Virtually all the Hebrew literature that has survived from OT times consists of the OT books themselves; and most subsequent writings, such as the Pseudepigrapha, the Qumran documents, and rabbinic literature, are dedicated to religious subjects. Art work, likewise, was largely confined to the decorations of the tabernacle and temple. There is good reason, however, to include a section on music in the present chapter. Although this form of art too was used primarily in connection with the worship of God, it is evident that musical activity was common more broadly in society (cf. Gen. 4:21; 31:27; 1 Sam. 16:16–17; Job 21:12; Lam. 5:14; Isa. 5:12; Ezek. 26:13).

The history of Israel's higher civilization in general and the organization of the musical service in the temple began with King David's reign. To him has been ascribed not only the creation and singing of the psalms, but also the provision of musical instruments (1 Chr. 23:5; 2 Chr. 7:6). King David chose the Levites to supply musicians for the holy temple. Out of the thirty thousand who were employed at this time, the impressive number of four thousand was selected for the musical service. Years later, when King Solomon had finished all work for the temple and brought in all the things David his father had dedicated, the priest and the congregation of Israel assembled before the ark, and the musical service was begun by the Levites (1 Chr. 25:6–7). Music played an important part also on the day of the dedication of the temple (2 Chr. 5:12–14).

Musicians in the Assyrian court (Ashurbanipal's palace in Nineveh, 7th cent. BC).

Z. Radovan/www.BibleLandPictures.com

In Solomon's temple the choir formed a distinct body. They were furnished homes and were on salary. Ezekiel says they had chambers between the walls and windows with southern views (Ezek. 40:44). The choir numbered two thousand singers and was divided into two choirs. The first examples in the Bible of antiphonal or responsive singing are the songs of Moses and Miriam after the passage through the Red Sea (Exod. 15).

The orchestra and the choir personnel were greatly reduced in the second temple. According to late Jewish literature, the orchestra consisted of a minimum of two harps and a maximum of six; a minimum of nine lyres, maximum limitless; a minimum of two oboes and a maximum of twelve; and one cymbal. The second temple choir consisted of a minimum of twelve adult singers, maximum limitless. The singers, all male, were between thirty and fifty years of age. Five years of musical training was a prerequisite to membership in the second temple choir. In addition to the male adults, sons of the Levites were permitted to participate in the choir "in order to add sweetness to the song."

The musical service in the temple at the time of Christ was essentially the same as that in King Solomon's temple, with the exception of a few minor changes in certain forms of singing. There were two daily services in the temple—the morning and evening sacrifices. After the sacrificial acts, the trumpet was sounded, which was the signal for the priests to prostrate themselves, but for the Levites it marked the beginning of the musical service. Two priests would now take their stand at the right and left of the altar and blow their silver trumpets. Afterward, these two priests would approach the cymbal player and take their stand beside him, one on the right and one on the left. When given a sign with a flag by the president, this Levite sounded his cymbal, and this was the sign for the Levites to begin singing a part of the daily psalm accompanied by instrumental music. Whenever they stopped singing, the priests would again blow their trumpets, and the people would prostrate themselves. Not only psalms were sung but also parts of the Pentateuch. The psalm of the day was sung in three sections, and at the close of each the priests would blow three fanfares on their silver trumpets, a signal for the congregation to bow down and worship the Lord.

In the daily service of the temple, both the morning and the evening sacrifice came to a close with the singing of a psalm. The real meaning of the headings of the various psalms is still veiled in darkness. Whether they indicate the names of the instruments employed in accompanying the psalms, or whether they refer to the tune to which they were sung, is still a problem for the musicologist. The word *selah*, which is found so frequently in the Psalms, is another expression that has not been satisfactorily explained. Whether it means an interlude, a pause, or a cadence is not known. Many scholars believe it indicates a musical interlude by the temple orchestra.

Several Hebrew words describe the joyous, rhythmic movements of the dance, which evidently played a significant part in Israelite life more generally. Dancing has been associated with war and hunting, with marriage, birth, and other occasions since human records began to be written. Throughout past ages, dancing has been linked with worship, and this activity was considered an integral part of the religious ceremonies in ancient Israel. In sacramental dance worshippers sought to express through bodily movements praise or penitence, worship or prayer. It has been accompanied by clapping of the hands. Percussion and other noise-making instruments seem to be native to dance (Jdg. 11:34; Ps. 68:25).

The Hebrew people developed their own type of dancing, associated in the main with worship. Basically, it was more like modern religious shouting by individuals or processions of exuberant groups. Dancing was usually done by women, with one of them leading, as in the case of Miriam, when a form of antiphonal singing was used (Exod. 15:20–21; cf. also Jdg. 21:20–23; 1 Sam. 18:6; Ps. 68:25). It usually took place out of doors. Men might dance solo, as in the case of David before the ark of the covenant (2 Sam. 6:14–16), and in groups, as when Israel celebrated the victory over the Amalekites (1 Sam. 30:16). That there is a time for dancing was recognized by the writer of Ecclesiastes (Eccl. 3:4). Job complained against the rich because of their ability to dance (Job 21:11). Jeremiah bemoaned the tragedy that made singing and dancing out of place (Lam. 5:15). The redemption of Israel was to be celebrated by dancing, with virgins and men and boys having part (Jer. 31:13). Religious dancing is mentioned only twice in Psalms (Pss. 149:3; 150:4).

Chapter 5

Government

The term *government* refers to the control and administration of public policy. The ancient nation of Israel was unique in that it was organized as a *theocracy* (a state ruled by divine guidance). Although the precise form of government varied during the nation's history, the underlying conviction was always there in the OT that the Lord is the true ruler of his people. Whoever exercised rule over the nation, the ultimate authority belonged to God. In NT times, the state was the Roman empire, paganistic and powerful, but Christians believed that even that authority was derived from God (Matt. 22:15–22; Rom. 13:1–7; 1 Pet. 2:17).

Towns and Cities

One normally thinks of the English word *town* as referring to something larger than a village but smaller than a city, yet in actual usage the distinctions often blur (as when we speak of Chicago as a town). In the Bible it is even more difficult to discriminate clearly between the relevant terms. The primary Hebrew word for "city" (*'îr*) can be applied to a place as large as Nineveh (Jon. 1:3), but it is also used very frequently of towns whose inhabitants could not have numbered more than a few hundred. The same is true of the corresponding Greek term (*polis*), which can be applied to Jerusalem (Matt. 4:5), but also to the small town of Nazareth (2:23). Both languages, however, use certain terms that specifically indicate unwalled settlements and dependent villages of a walled city (e.g., the settlements surrounding Heshbon, Num. 21:25; cf. also Neh. 11:25–30; Matt. 9:35; et al.).

According to Lev. 25:29–31, "villages without walls" come under a different law of redemption (in cases where individuals had to sell their property because of financial difficulties): the houses in those villages were to be returned to the sellers in the Jubilee Year, whereas city houses could not be redeemed if more than a year passed from the time of sale. In the OT period, the city was distinguished by having a defensive wall as well as being the center of commerce and industry and, in some cases, the place where the local governor lived. In the NT period, a town was considered a city if it possessed a constitution and law differing from country law and following the law of the crown.

Towns were principally agricultural centers, dependent on walled cities for protection and for the sale and exchange of farm produce. Buildings were of lower quality, often crude. In distinction from a major town or city, the unwalled village was easy prey for conquest, having no defensive facilities such as moats, towers, or fortified gates (Ezek. 38:11). When threatened, the villagers thronged into the city, increasing the danger of famine (cf. 2 Ki. 6:24–29). From Hebron northward a gradual increase of villages occurred toward and beyond Jerusalem, with the greatest number being found in the territory of the tribe of Zebulun, in Lower Galilee, where rainfall was greatest. In NT times the Roman army made this area a peaceful territory where the people lived without fear, and agriculture and industry flourished in its many villages. Upper Galilee was too broken and too wooded to support the agriculture necessary to village life.

Local village government was administered through the elders who also acted as judges (Ruth 4:2), but the villages were under the larger jurisdiction of the towns (cf. Josh. 15:20–62; 18:24, 28; et al.). The scene of these frequent functions was the city gate, at times provided with benches. The size of villages varied according to whether the country was farmed intensively or not. In the agricultural centers, grain was threshed within the confines of the villages. Activity increased at harvest time, but many of the villagers would be away with the herds at other times.

The rise of cities has been termed the second great "revolution" of civilization. Unlike the earliest revolution—the domestication of plants and animals in Neolithic agriculture—the origins of urban life were more expressive of changes in the interaction of human beings with one another than in the interaction with their physical environment. Of course, to make urban life possible, the concept of surplus food, its production, and accumulation had first to be invented and valued.

But the essential element that distinguished the town or city from village life was the invention, development, and diffusion of a whole series of new institutions in greater size and more complex social character. The most significant criterion of urban life was the expansion of full-time specialists in nonagricultural activities. By such criteria, it appears likely that the first towns originated in Mesopotamia soon after 3500 BC. The steps in the transformation of the older village settlements into cities, a process that took many centuries, may be traceable in a number of sites. Typically, these towns grew up around a walled precinct containing a temple area that was devoted to the main city-god and other deities.

The excavated remains of Megiddo; aerial view from west.

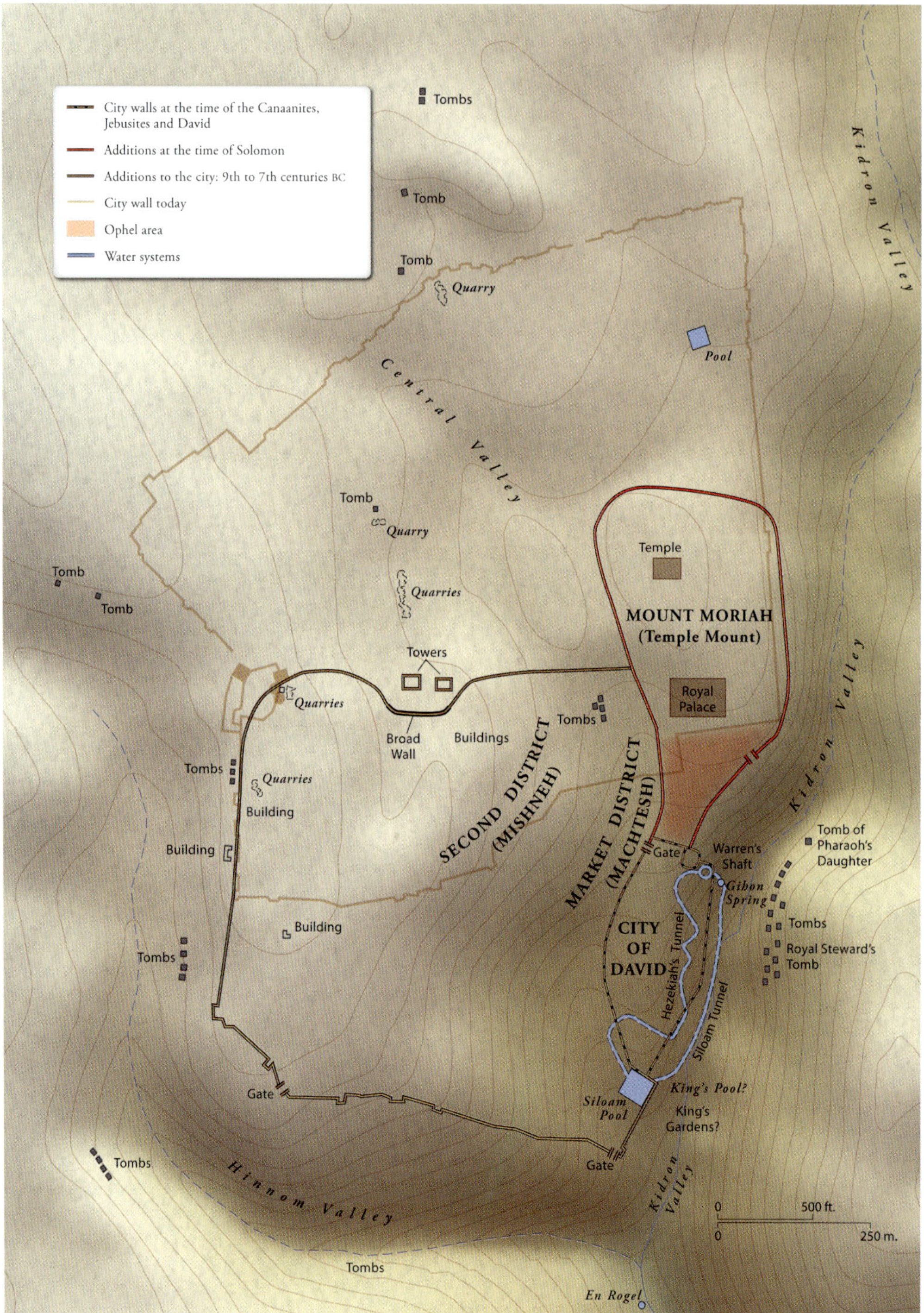

Old Testament Jerusalem.

The earliest Palestinian town to be discovered thus far is Jericho. Although the site may have been inhabited as early as 9000 BC, an actual town, some nine acres in extent, developed only around 4500 BC. The first significant period of town formation, however, took place about 2,000 years later. The great population centers were in the valleys, especially along the important coastal route. Most towns were five to ten acres in size, but some covered as many as fifty acres. Around 1700 BC, large towns with strong fortifications began to be built. The largest of them was Hazor, located some ten miles north of the Sea of Galilee (Josh. 11:1, 10–13, et al.); it occupied an immense rectangular area of over 175 acres, surrounded by a huge ramp.

Generally, the high density of towns in the coastal plain was such that each town ruled a small hinterland. The more isolated towns in the interior hill lands tended to have a different political control of larger territories, often with a capital such as Shechem or Jerusalem controlling lesser towns and villages as well within its sphere of influence. Presumably, considerable areas of the interior hill lands were still forested and unoccupied.

Following the Israelite settlement in the land, the Hebrew tribes changed their way of life from dwellings in booths and tents, following the herds and flocks, to settled agriculture and town life. Sometimes, as at Bethel, an Israelite settlement was built upon the ruins of the Canaanite city soon after its destruction. Elsewhere the evidence suggests Israelite foundation of new settlements (e.g., Gibeah and Ramah, a short distance north of Jerusalem). There is also evidence of small permanent settlements created in mountainous terrain, formerly forested, in Upper Galilee and elsewhere.

By the use of the water cistern and the deforestation of the interior hills, the Israelites created a new pattern of settlement. Now this area became a new focus of urban life, and Jerusalem eventually came into its own. The contrast between the strongly fortified Canaanite cities of the coast and the small, poorly defended Israelite settlements at the beginning of the conquest of the land was later reinforced by the invasion of the Philistines from the sea. Their threat led to concerted action from the Israelite tribes, resulting in the founding of the monarchy and, later, the establishment of Jerusalem as a national capital in the eighth year of David's reign.

The significance of Jerusalem as a royal capital was its federal standing. Originally a Jebusite fortress, it was captured by David, and so it was neutral territory in relation to all of the rival tribes, each of whom might have quarreled over the choice of the site of the national capital. Hebron, David's first capital (2 Sam. 5:5), could never have provided the necessary cohesion. Later, Samaria became the capital of the northern kingdom (1 Ki. 4:7–19).

Compared to the 1,800 acres of Nineveh and even the 240 acres of Carchemish, the cities of the OT in Palestine were small. However, there is the archaeological problem of identifying the walls and actual sites of many of the ancient towns. For example, there is still little positive evidence for the course of the walls of Jerusalem until post-biblical times. The "fortress of Zion" or "City of David" (2 Sam. 5:7) was on the southeastern hill, covering no more than fifteen acres, which suggests a population of about 3,000 (approximately the size of such other important cities as Taanach and Megiddo). By the time of Hezekiah, Jerusalem had expanded considerably (see chap. 4, section on Population).

The citadel of Arad.

www.HolyLandPhotos.org

Four characteristics of the biblical cities help to explain their sites, locations, and shapes.

(a) First was the stronghold character of so many of the towns. The walled fortifications of cities are often impressive, and larger settlements had their "strong tower" inside the city (e.g., Thebes, Jdg. 9:50–51). There are frequent allusions to the high walls, towers, and gates of the city (Num. 13:28; Deut. 3:5; Josh. 2:5, 15; 6:5; Neh. 3:1–3, 11, 25). The gate was a massive structure, often with a room over the gateway (2 Sam. 18:33) and with guards on the roof of the towers and gateways (18:24; 2 Ki. 9:17). The city walls were very thick; a width of twenty to thirty feet was not unusual.

At Shechem, a most impressive city, excavations have revealed a sequence of walls that well illustrates the technology of fortification. The earliest walls (before the Israelite occupation) were freestanding brick structures on stone sockets, about nine feet thick. These were succeeded by great earthen embankments and then followed by massive walls with great stone boulders. In the course of these stages of fortification, the configuration of the natural contours of these typical hilltop towns was altered significantly: the top was leveled for the town itself, while the slopes deliberately steepened and flanked with great artificial ramps.

(b) In contrast to the impressive works of fortification, the houses of Palestinian towns were generally small, and the streets were very narrow. The street layout was a maze of crooked causeways and blind alleys. The only broad places (Neh. 8:1, 3, 16; Jer. 5:1) were at the intersection of main roads and especially near the city gates. At these public places, notably at the city gate, public business was transacted, law cases adjudicated, and markets held (Gen. 23:10; Ruth 4:1–11; 2 Sam. 15:2; 1 Ki. 22:10; 2 Ki. 7:1; Neh. 8:1). Some streets were devoted to bazaars (1 Ki. 20:34; Jer. 37:21).

(c) A third trait of Palestinian towns was the sanctity of sites, either as the origin of the settlement or because of a long association with the town. "High places" or sanctuaries were commonly associated in Canaanite times with the veneration of springs of water and mountaintops, both topographic features of significance for later urban populations. At Gezer, Taanach, and other excavated sites, rock surfaces pitted with cup marks of a sacrificial function have been laid bare, flanked by pillars of unhewn stone (Deut. 12:3; Hos. 10:1).

(d) Finally, as water supply in an arid or semiarid climate was so essential, one or more springs in the vicinity of these towns was vital (Gen. 24:11). Mesha king of Moab narrates in the Moabite Stone: "And there was no cistern inside the town at Qarhoh, so I said to all the people: 'Let each of you make a cistern in his house!'" Such private systems of cisterns are characteristic of later places like Qumran, Masada, and other excavated sites of eastern Judea. Conduits and water tunnels too are typical of the Iron Age fortresses such as those discovered at Megiddo, Shechem, and Jerusalem. These were built for impressive distances, linking springs outside the defense system into the city and becoming a standard technique for chariot fortresses (2 Ki. 20:20).

The ancient Jewish village of Katzrin (in the Golan Heights) included a synagogue.

Edom/Wikimedia Commons

Aerial view of Caesarea.

Wikimedia Commons

After the OT period, many of the Palestinian towns lost their fortification walls and were in ruins. When the Romans took control of the country after 63 BC and the great town builder King Herod held office, cities were transformed and several created. Samaria, renamed Sebaste (Augusta), was reconstructed with new walls and towers enclosing an irregular oval nearly five-eighths of a mile in width. A huge temple over 225 feet long was built, with the Forum on the east side of the temple. Caesarea, on the coast between Mount Carmel and Joppa, took twelve years to build (25–13 BC). For most of the period between AD 6 and 66, Caesarea was the seat of the Roman government in the country. Here Paul was tried before Festus and Herod Agrippa (Acts 25–26).

By the time of Christ, the central fort of the city of Jerusalem was no longer on the hill south of the temple area, where it had been in OT times. A new wall had been built to enclose growth to the north of the old city. Still another wall was begun in the reign of Herod Agrippa to enclose the suburb farther to the north, which Josephus calls Bezetha. It was only completed two decades later, however. The topography of Jerusalem also changed. For example, the Tyropoeon Valley, which used to separate the eastern from the western sections of the city, was filled up partially with the refuse of centuries.

In addition, Herod the Great rebuilt a Maccabean fortress at the point where the second city wall approached the temple enclosure and named it Antonia, in honor of Mark Antony. The court of the Antonia is paved with huge limestone blocks; this may be what is called "the Stone Pavement" (Jn. 19:13). The Tower of Antonia was the place where Paul was imprisoned when he was rescued from the mob in the temple (Acts 21:30). Herod also rebuilt the temple and provided it with an enlarged courtyard, the southeastern part of which had to be supported by columns and immense vaults. A massive retaining wall was also built by Herod, of which the "Wailing Wall" on the west is typical (at least in its lower section). The temple itself was one of the most magnificent in the classical world.

A distinct group of NT cities are the Hellenistic towns that came into existence in the third and second centuries BC in Transjordan (east of the Jordan River) and at Scythopolis (Beth Shan). With the coming of the Romans, these ten cities were banded together into the Decapolis and placed under the political control of the Roman governor in Syria. The strategic importance of this eastern flank of the Roman frontier, along with the preservation of Hellenistic vis-à-vis Semitic and Jewish interests, explains their identity (Matt. 4:25; Mk. 5:20; 7:31). Among the best known of these towns are Gerasa (Jerash) and Philadelphia (Amman), laid out as typical Hellenistic cities.

Typical of the narrative of the Gospels is the rural atmosphere of Judea and of the tetrarchies administered under the house of Herod and the procurators. In the villages, a clerk administered the community as an official of the central government. The judge in the gospel narratives is also a feature of the Judean administration, doing what he likes in a very un-Roman and un-Greek way (Matt. 5:25; Lk. 12:58). Above him is the king, a petty tyrant, belonging to a world of satraps and other small rulers. That is to say, the Judean atmosphere of the Gospels is one of peasantry ruled by a succession of conquerors and their dependent princes. Towns were a matter of size rather than of a distinct form of government in the transitional period from the end of the second century BC to the end of the first century AD.

In the civic atmosphere of the Acts and the Epistles, a very different structure is felt. There is seen the classical Greek city development, where the people of the *polis* run their own municipal affairs, administered within their own territory. Their city councils are large, with more than five hundred members in each major city. Citizens are enfranchised, and the sense of justice for the rights of the individual is reinforced in city life. However, whereas the Roman cities of the western Mediterranean were by NT times an extension of Rome itself, the cities in the east were more provincial, more Hellenistic in culture, with often only a minority of Romans in the cities, sometimes constituting a town within a town.

Some of the cities visited by Paul, such as Antioch of Pisidia, Lystra, and Corinth have as many Greeks and Jews as Romans in their streets (Acts 13:14; 16:2; 18:4). It is primarily within these Hellenized cities that the spread of Christianity takes place in a strategic awareness of the privileges and opportunities for the dissemination of the faith in self-contained communities. Possibly most of the early Christians were concentrated in Asia Minor, where Jewish urban communities had long been established in trading centers and had created around them a circle of "God-fearing" Gentiles. It was in these latter circles that the Christian gospel took effect.

In contrast to the urban centers of Palestine, the cities mentioned in Acts were very diverse in character. One could find (a) a rigid bureaucracy in Roman military towns and colonial cities, (b) the more open character of the Greek city states, each with its own character, and (c) the hybrid features of the oriental cities of Asia Minor and Syria. Hints of diverse environmental detail are touched upon in the letters to the seven churches (Rev. 1–3). In addition, these cities were typically much larger, many of them formally planned either in Hellenistic or Roman style. These factors provided a growing complexity of detail in the urban life of Christian missionary enterprise.

Elders and Officials

In Israel, the elders were adult men who gathered in popular assembly or as a kind of council in every village. They also served as local rulers. Usually they were the heads of families, but probably were selected also on the basis of age, wisdom, ability, respect, or prowess. It is difficult to determine if the "officials" (KJV, "princes," e.g., Jdg. 8:6) were equivalent to the elders. Pharaoh had his elders (Gen. 50:7), and so did the Midianites and Moabites (Num. 22:7) and the Gibeonites (Josh. 9:11).

The origin of the elders in Hebrew history goes back to the nomadic period before the occupation of Palestine, with the roots of the office probably in the individual home within the clan. The elders were already recognized as a part of the community during the period of bondage in Egypt (Exod. 3:16; 4:29). It was the elders (obviously the heads of the houses) who were instructed concerning the observance of the first Passover in Egypt whereby the people might escape death (12:21). They were particularly associated with religious leadership (24:1, 9), including the offering of sacrifices (Lev. 4:15). Seventy elders were selected to share with Moses the burden of the people and were given part of the Spirit that rested on Moses (Num. 11:16–17). Elders are often mentioned alongside the priests (1 Ki. 8:3). There is one mention of elders of the priests (2 Ki. 19:2).

The elders served in various capacities. A principal function was to serve as judges in disputes or to dispense justice as they sat in the gates of the city (Deut. 22:15). The prophets demanded that respect for justice at the gate be shown (Amos 5:10–12; Zech. 8:16) and charged that the elders had become corrupt in their administration of justice. As members of what amounted to a popular court, the elders were not to bear false witness, accept gifts, or follow the majority in defiance of justice. Their responsibility was to condemn the guilty and acquit the innocent.

Each town had its own elders (Deut. 19:12), who determined if a criminal should be turned over to the avenger to die, thus depriving him of the protection of the cities of refuge. They determined whether a rebellious son should be stoned to death, and they participated in the execution of the sentence (21:18–21). They also adjudged the validity of a husband's charge that his bride was not a virgin (22:15). They settled cases concerning levirate law when a man did not want to marry his deceased brother's wife (25:7–10). The elders also served as witnesses to commercial transactions (Ruth 4:4) and as military leaders (Josh. 8:10; 1 Sam. 4:3).

Elders were involved in the selection of kings of the nation. They demanded that Samuel appoint for them their first king (1 Sam. 8:4–5) and participated in the anointing of David as king over all Israel after the death of Saul (2 Sam. 3:17; 5:3). It is most likely that it was the elders who gathered at Shechem after the death of Solomon to receive certain assurances from Rehoboam before recognizing him as king. They apparently did not acknowledge the right of automatic succession by inheritance (1 Ki. 12). When Jezebel plotted the death of Naboth, she wrote the elders and nobles of Jezreel to provide false witnesses in order that Naboth might be stoned to death (1 Ki. 21:8–11). Through the wise counsel of the elders, Jeremiah's life was saved by remembering the prophecies of Micah (Jer. 26:16–19).

Nothing is said about the organization of the councils of the elders of the tribes. Their number probably depended on the size of the local community; there were seventy-seven at Succoth (Jdg. 8:14). It is quite unlikely that there was a council of elders of the entire nation selected from the elders of the various tribes. The elders seemed to occupy a continuing place of importance throughout the history of Israel, from their sojourn in Egypt to the postexilic period, when mention was made that they gave orders to assemble the people to deal with the question of foreign marriages (Ezra 10:8).

Even in NT times, elders still exercised judicial authority and are mentioned alongside the chief priests as taking leadership in the trial and arrest of Jesus (e.g., Matt. 26:3, 47; 27:1). We read also that the Jewish "rulers, the elders and the teachers of the law," along with the high priest's family, were in charge of questioning Paul and John after their arrest (Acts 4:5–6). Later the chief priests and elders brought charges against Paul before the Roman governor (25:15).

At the higher, national level of the royal court in Israel, the king had "his attendants, his nobles and his officials" (2 Ki. 24:12). We read also that King David had a "counselor" (Ahithophel, 2 Sam. 15:12).

A special role was played by those who were given the title of *sopher*, "scribe." In the ancient world, relatively few people received the training necessary to gain skill in the art of writing, and those who followed the scribal profession were usually regarded as scholars and could hold high civic offices. In ancient Israel the scribal craft was principally confined to certain clans who doubtless preserved the trade as a family guild profession, passing the knowledge of this essential skill from father to son (1 Chr. 2:55).

During the united and later Judean monarchies a substantial number of scribes came from the Levites. The point of contact between the ritual and scribal functions derives from the demand for fiscal organization of temple operations (e.g., in Mesopotamia and Egypt most of the earliest writings are associated with temple records). A Levite recorded the priestly assignments (1 Chr. 24:6), and the royal scribe helped in counting the public funds collected for the repair of the temple (2 Ki. 12:10–11; 2 Chr. 14:11). Since the furnishing of written copies of the law was a (scribal) Levitical responsibility (Deut. 17:18), the reforms of Jehoshaphat (cf. 2 Chr. 17) cannot be disassociated from the scribal function.

Statue of a seated Egyptian scribe.

Scribes may have served as counselors (e.g., 1 Chr. 27:32) or borne the responsibility for mustering the army (2 Ki. 25:19). The highest-ranking government scribe was the royal secretary. His position in the cabinet is difficult to judge, since ministerial lists may not be given in sequence of rank. If, however, the members of David's cabinet are listed in sequence in 2 Sam. 8:16–18, the royal secretary ranked below the top military commander, the recorder, and the two chief priests, but above the commander over special forces.

The hierarchy may have been different during the divided monarchies, since the scribe or secretary is twice listed between the recorder and the palace administrator (2 Ki. 18:18, 37; cf. Isa. 36:3, 22); here he served as one of three ministers appointed to negotiate with Sennacherib, who demanded the surrender of Jerusalem. Moreover, by

Josiah's reign, the scribe Shaphan preceded both the recorder and "the ruler of the city" (cf. 2 Ki. 22:3–13 with 2 Chr. 34:8–21), suggesting that the relationship between scribe and recorder had been reversed since David's era. Royal scribes had offices (Jer. 36:12) that were evidently located in the building complex of the royal Judean palace, serving to illustrate the high standing of the king's secretary in the government. See also chap. 6 (section on Scribes and Rabbis.)

The King

In the system of the ancient religious state, patriotism and religious piety were synonymous. To oust or overthrow the legitimate king was to commit treason against the state cult. Unless a new administration could gain the ritual approval of the hierarchy of the cult and the necessary legitimization of the city gods, it would be the victim of a counterrevolution that often degenerated into fratricidal feuds and harem intrigues.

This crown, made of copper, was discovered in the Cave of the Treasures in the Judean Desert.

Z. Radovan/www.BibleLandPictures.com

Throughout the long centuries of Egypt's history, and sporadically in Mesopotamia, the gods were considered royalty and the rulers as divine. In Syria-Palestine and other border areas of the great river valley civilizations, the kings served as the high priests of the cult. Even in imperial Rome, the grandest of the Caesar's honorific titles was *pontifex maximus* (literally, "greatest bridge-maker," the highest priestly office). The approval of the town deities was of such importance that conquerors, with mock reverence, often listed the gods of captive regions in the place of geographic names. In fact it was the obeisance of the conqueror to these deities that could establish his right to the local authority even though the gods along with their towns had been captured.

The historic establishment of kingship in Israel would seem to be a contradiction of the principle that the nation was peculiarly under Yahweh's providence. The judge Samuel, acting in the prophetic office, clearly declared the extent of the liability that such an earthly monarch would prove to be. After listing the avaricious requirements of a royal establishment, Samuel adds, "When that day comes, you will cry out for relief from the king you have chosen, and the LORD will not answer you in that day" (1 Sam. 8:18).

The kingship of Yahweh had been expressly stated in Moses' first discourse from Sinai: "Now if you obey me fully and keep my covenant, then out of all nations you will be my treasured possession. Although the whole earth is mine, you will be for me a kingdom of priests and a holy nation" (Exod. 19:5–6). It was this aspect of God's sovereignty over Israel that the nation rejected when they asked for a king. As God said to Samuel, "Listen to all that the people are saying to you; it is not you they have rejected, but they have rejected me as their king" (1 Sam. 8:7). Even the perverse desire for kingship in Israel was constructed in terms of the law of God, although it manifested itself as a rejection of his law.

The previous period of the judges had been one of conflict between the migrant and tribal people of Israel and the loose-knit confederacy of Canaanite city-states. During the time preceding the exodus from Egypt, the Israelites had confronted the monolithic façade of the Egyptian religious state. As Egypt lost its Asiatic provinces, the Philistines pushed southward and Israel settled the land. In time the small states and trading villages of Syria-Palestine coalesced into petty monarchies and ultimately into dynasties. The achievement of Saul, David, and Solomon was not a novelty nor did it take place in a vacuum, but it was paralleled by centralization of authority elsewhere at that time and in that area.

Kings and kingship are first mentioned in the OT in the narrative of the battle fought by Abraham with a number of rulers (Gen. 14). Even the pharaohs of Egypt during the time of Israel's sojourn are called "kings." After the conquest, settlement, and solidification of the tribal organization of Israel in Canaan, the judges became the legal and executive authorities of the twelve tribes. Even though a number of judges were also prophets, the judgeship was not an anointed office (1 Sam. 15:10), and thus it served no direct messianic function in the Israelite theocracy.

Samuel acted as a prophet in selecting and anointing Saul as the first king of Israel (1 Sam. 11:15). It is basic to the OT concept of kingship to recognize the necessity of the prophetic office. The prophet as spokesman for Yahweh assented to the people's request for a king, determined who should be king, and then marked him as a person of messianic character by anointing him. Therefore no king could claim legitimacy without the prophetic approval and its divine investiture. The impossibility of the royal line being infiltrated by foreigners or compromised from outside the community of Israel was assured. The later history of the Hebrew monarchy demonstrates the frequency with which the prophets rejected the iniquitous infatuation of the kings with Gentile and pagan royalty. For this reason both Persia and Greece found it necessary to unseat the monarchy totally and to replace it with an authority based on their own culture, whereas in other civilizations they conquered they were able to gain the legitimization of the ancient cult.

In most of the nations thriving in the first millennium BC, the rulers were chosen from a large group of pretenders, either by the officials of the state cult or by some settlement among the aristocratic families. In Israel it was the choice and direction of Yahweh that determined the successor to the throne, though a process of drawing by lots may have been involved (1 Sam. 10:21; cf. NRSV). The prophetic anointing of the king not only indicated the messianic character of the Hebrew ruler, but it imparted to him divine authority demanding the obedience of the people (11:7).

The king, like the prophet and the priest, was sacrosanct but never sacerdotal (1 Sam. 24:6). Even the members of the royal house and potential future kings were accorded reverence, as in the case of the boy Joash (2 Ki. 11:2–3). The families of former rulers were shown certain honors (cf. the benefits King David bestowed upon Mephibosheth, the grandson of Saul, 2 Sam. 9:6–10). This respect reached even to the pagan relatives of

The Gihon Spring, where Solomon was anointed king (1 Kings 1:38–39).

Todd Bolen/www.BiblePlaces.com

a slain ruler, as in the case of the murdered Jezebel, concerning whose body Jehu commanded, "Take care of that cursed woman ... and bury her, for she was a king's daughter" (2 Ki. 9:34).

On the other hand, the divine approval of either king or royalty could be removed, and this decision too would be indicated to the king by the prophet (1 Sam. 16:14). Unlike other monarchs of antiquity, the Hebrew king was not an absolute autocrat. Like the humblest commoner, he was subject to the Mosaic legislation (Deut. 17:18–20).

Since the character of Israelite kingship was defined largely by the customs of the nations round about Canaan, in the same manner the duties and privileges of the Jewish rulers followed the ancient traditions. The customary ancient Near Eastern monarch possessed a palace, was installed upon a throne, and had access to a harem of wives and concubines. In time all these aspects became a part of the Hebrew monarchical establishment.

Although the ultimate symbol among most of the ancients was the scepter, no such instrument is ever described or associated with a Jewish king. In an age when livery was considered of great importaance, the royal garments of Israel are described as an outer robe or vestment befitting rank (1 Ki. 22:10, 30) and the usual cloak or under-mantle (1 Sam. 24:4, 11) of the highest quality (1 Chr. 15:27; 2 Sam. 13:18). Two types of metallic ornaments are mentioned: the chaplets or fillets (2 Sam. 1:10) and the crown or diadem, which in Zechariah's time was made of silver and gold, possibly electrum (Zech. 6:11).

The maintenance of more than one wife must have been a feature of the monarchy, and in the latter times the oriental harem appeared in Israel. In time the custom of political marriage, whereby a king would certify a treaty by marriage into the allied nation's royal family, became common in Israel. Solomon and his followers adhered to this tradition, and it was this contradiction of the divine commandment that led to the marriage of Ahab and Jezebel, so that later a pagan princess, their daughter Athaliah, became queen.

The kings were accompanied by groups of retainers who acted as a bodyguard. Chief among these were the family detachments known as the Kerethites, Pelethites, and Gittites (2 Sam. 15:18). In the eighth chapter of 2 Samuel are listed the officers of David's court: Joab the general of the army; Jehoshaphat the recorder, a sort of chief adviser; Zadok and Ahimelech the priests; Seraiah the scribe; Benaiah the chief of the bodyguard; and the princes of the palace who served as David's ministers. It is safe to assume that this list gives only the names of the king's cabinet and that there were armor-bearers (1 Sam. 16:21) and other military officials as well as a large group of cooks, wine stewards, butlers, tailors, and other such official craftsmen.

This inscribed stone from the 9th cent. BC records a land grant by a Babylonian king to a priest.

Like other regents, the kings of Israel had the authority to levy taxes and collect tribute from their subjects (1 Ki. 4:6–21). Subject kingdoms and peoples under Israel's sovereignty paid their annual tribute in the same way as when Israel itself was a suzerain of Assyria under Hezekiah (2 Ki. 18:15–16). Wealth was counted in material stores of gems, garments, precious metals, and livestock (2 Chr. 32:27–29). Opulence and magnificence were determined by the number of servants and retainers a king could command and support, as well as the style of dress, food, and appointments in which he kept them (2 Chr. 31:16–19).

Taxation was mostly in kind, and the royal flocks, herds, and vineyards were tended by work corvées made up of the citizenry. The international trade was also in terms of goods and produce, most of which came from the royal forests and mines (1 Ki. 5:10–11). However, because of the Mosaic law, which bound even the kings of Israel, the right of commandeering except for military necessity was forbidden.

In the full perspective of the thousands of years of Jewish history, the monarchy actually involved a brief duration. Under the early rulers—Saul, David, and Solomon—the spirit of conquest was still lively enough to advance the kingdom territorially and

The bull-god Apis holding the solar disk and the uraeus (sacred asp).

Marie-Lan Nguyen/Wikimedia Commons

materially to its greatest extent. Even this period of ascendancy above the neighboring petty states of the East Mediterranean coast lasted a scant century. After the division of the kingdom under Rehoboam and Jeroboam, the political power of the Jewish monarchy declined until in about two hundred years' time Israel, the northern regency, had not the resources to forestall its destruction before Assyria (722 BC). Judah, the more stable principality, lingered on until 586 BC, when Jerusalem fell to Babylon.

Law and Justice

There are two distinct forms clearly discernible in Israel's law, even when broken into the smallest possible units. The first form, usually called categoric or apodictic (expressing absolute certainty), is best illustrated in the format of the first part of each of the Ten Commandments. It is characterized by its terseness and abruptness, and it involves an absolute command, apparently admitting no exceptions. The same idea may be expressed with the pattern, "The one who [does such-and-such] must surely die [literally, 'dying he will be put to death']" (cf. Exod. 21:12 and following verses).

The second type of law to be found in the Torah is casuistic, that is, case-law. It normally introduces an instance, ending with a "then ..." clause. Such laws should not be regarded as hypothetical instances, but as actual precedents or case judgments. It is in these areas that Israel's case-law approaches most closely that of her immediate Semitic neighbors. This is natural enough, since, given roughly similar levels of civilization and circumstances of life, similar problems were liable to arise and broadly similar solutions to be found (although Israel's law is consistently more humane). Semitic law is most familiar to modern scholars in the codification associated with Hammurabi of Babylon.

Bronze bull from Late Bronze Hazor.

Todd Bolen/www.BiblePlaces.com

With regard to content, Israel's laws throughout are dominated by the revelation of God received at Mount Sinai. There is a humaneness, an avoidance of mutilations and other savage punishments, and an awareness of the value of human personality and the individual, for which we would search in vain in other codes. This, and not any outward form, is the distinctiveness of Israel's law. One example will suffice: the small space given in Israel's code to property laws, and the large space given to personal relations. Moreover, even in the case of the land laws the motivation for every law is strongly personal and religious.

Biblical jurisprudence was based upon the assumption that human beings are under obligation to carry out the revealed will of God in leading a holy life, respecting the rights of God and neighbor, not simply for pragmatic reasons, but rather as creatures made in the likeness of God. This obligation was regarded as unchangeable and absolute, beyond human authority to amend or even to adapt to some general standard prevailing in current society.

Broadly speaking, the Mosaic legislation dealt with two main types of offense: the religious and the civil. Crimes against God, which usually called for death by stoning, included idolatry (the worship of other gods, e.g., Exod. 20:3–6; 22:20), infant sacrifice (Lev. 20:2), witchcraft and related practices (Exod. 22:18; Deut. 18:10–11), blasphemy (Exod. 20:7; Lev. 24:11–23), false prophecy (Deut. 18:20–22), Sabbath-breaking (Exod. 20:9–10, 31:13–17), and explicit defiance of the authority of God's law (Num. 15:30–31).

With regard to civil offenses, the Mosaic legislation does not clearly distinguish between crimes and torts. A *crime* is an offense directly or indirectly against the public, of sufficient gravity to be dealt with through judicial proceedings, brought by representatives of the public interest. Crimes against human beings consisted of offenses of such gravity as to endanger society or the state. They went beyond matters of controversy between private individuals,

This monument, discovered in Ras Shamra (Ugarit), depicts the Canaanite storm-god Baal with a thunderbolt (c. 14th cent. BC).

Marie-Lan Nguyen/Wikimedia Commons

This scale, used for weighing gold and silver, dates to the Roman period.

Z. Radovan/www.BibleLandPictures.com

posing a threat to the safety of the community as a whole. They included homicide (Exod. 20:13; Num. 35:31), assault (Exod. 21:26–27), robbery (20:15; Lev. 6:2–7), sex crimes (Exod. 20:14; Lev. 18:6–23; 20:10–21), dishonor to parents (Exod. 20:12; 21:15, 17), kidnapping (21:16), malicious prosecution and perjury (20:16; Deut. 19:16–20). A *tort*, on the other hand, is an offense against an individual for which the latter may recover damages for the injury incurred. Torts involved property damage (Exod. 22:5–6; Lev. 24:18, 21), bailments (Exod. 22:9–11), and oppression of the underprivileged (22:21–24).

Since there were no regularly appointed public prosecutors in ancient judicial practice, it normally devolved upon the victims of injustice, or their nearest surviving relative, to bring criminal cases to the attention of the judges in the jurisdiction where the crime occurred. Even in the case of murder, the nearest surviving male relative had the responsibility of "kinsman-redeemer" and acted as prosecutor, or even as executioner, of the murderer; so also with the lesser offenses. This practice tended to confuse the distinction between torts and crimes.

International Relations

From its very beginnings the history of Israel was characterized by international conflict, for it involved both the Hebrews' escape from Egyptian slavery and their military occupation of Canaanite land, leading to the somewhat chaotic period of the "judges," an extended time of confrontation with neighboring peoples.

It was only after the establishment of the monarchy, with Saul as its first king (c. 1040 BC), that Israel could begin to develop political unity. During the reign of the next monarch, David, the nation established itself as a significant player in the international scene, as is evident, for example, from David's relationship with the kings of Tyre and Hamath (2 Sam. 5:10–12; 8:9–10).

International relationships flourished dramatically when Solomon became king. One of his first alliances was with Egypt. It involved taking an Egyptian princess as a queen (1 Ki. 3:1), and gaining the town of Gezer (9:16) was hardly full compensation; future trade relations with Egypt proved valuable.

A treaty of special worth was forged with the Phoenician king of Tyre, Hiram, who had been a close friend of David. Hiram was ruler of an extensive maritime domain, possessed rich natural resources, and had highly skilled artisans. Solomon drew heavily on all three for his building operations and his own shipping enterprise (1 Ki. 5:1–12; 9:10–14). In the course of time, Solomon released to Hiram twenty cities in Galilee, some think to pay a deficit in what Solomon had purchased, though others think that it was for a loan (2 Chr. 8:1–2 seems to say that Solomon got the cities back again). In addition, the biblical text (1 Ki. 10:24–25 = 2 Chr. 9:23–24) points to a network of treaties with countries of all sizes, and many of his wives seem to have been sureties for these treaties. One of these wives, an Ammonite, was the mother of Rehoboam, the next king (1 Ki. 14:21).

Trade considerations were closely tied to the political alliances that were forged. The king of Israel held a pivotal position because he controlled the main route along the sea and the main route east of Jordan, both of which connected the nations of the south with the nations to the north. Solomon was able not only to tax goods that passed along these routes but also to act profitably as a middleman in the trade deals. Solomon particularly loved horse trading and set up an arrangement in which he procured chariots

In this panel from the Black Obelisk (9th cent. BC), King Jehu of Israel is shown bowing to Shalmaneser III of Assyria.

Z. Radovan/www.BibleLandPictures.com

and horses from Egypt and Kue (in Cilicia) and sold them to other nations. Egypt had to get wood for the chariots from areas that Solomon controlled, so he had a virtual stranglehold on the industry (1 Ki. 10:28–29).

Solomon's relationship with Hiram of Tyre was not limited to buying lumber and securing skillful workers for building projects; Solomon was also able to exploit Hiram's maritime knowledge for his own advantage. Ships and sailors were obtained for a fleet that operated out of Ezion Geber (on the Gulf of Aqabah). This fleet made trade contacts with Arabia and the eastern coast of Africa, bringing many strange and exotic goods and animals to Israel. Closely related to the shipping port was a mining and refinery project that exploited the rich copper deposits near Ezion Geber. Remains of the mining operations have been found there by archaeologists. The copper and bronze produced had ready buyers in other parts of the world. It would seem that Hiram's Mediterranean fleet could distribute widely these metals (1 Ki. 9:26, 28; 10:11–12, 22).

The celebrated visit of the queen of Sheba was as much a trade mission as a trip motivated by a strong curiosity about the reputed wisest man in the world. Her elaborate gifts could serve as "samples" of what her country could offer to aggressive traders (1 Ki. 10:1–10, 13; 2 Chr. 9:1–9, 12). Thus the combination of fairly peaceful relations with other nations, dominance of Canaan (the "land bridge" of the ancient Near East), and the effective control of the major land trade routes poured wealth into Israel at a spectacular rate. Gold, silver, and cedar were no longer rarities in Jerusalem. But Solomon's extravagance strained the income to the limit; a fiscal deficit was not unknown even in the "Golden Age."

Soon after the death of Solomon, the nation divided into a northern kingdom (known as Israel or Ephraim) and a southern kingdom (Judah, which preserved the Davidic dynasty). Both of them continued relations with surrounding countries, sometimes peaceful and sometimes hostile. The northern kingdom in particular expanded its influence under Omri, who reigned c. 885–874 BC and who, among other things, established stronger ties with Phoenicia. This relationship served to increase the prestige and wealth of Israel, but at a cost. Omri's son, Ahab, married the Phoenician princess Jezebel, who promoted the worship of Baal, thus weakening the religious and cultural fabric of Israelite society.

Warfare

Much of the history of the Hebrew monarchies was characterized by military conflict, especially with the rise of the great ancient empires. The Assyrian nation eventually conquered the kingdom of Israel, capturing its capital, Samaria, in 722 BC. More than a century later, the Babylonian empire overwhelmed Palestine, and Jerusalem fell in 586. It is therefore appropriate to take account of the nature of warfare at the time.

In the ancient world two types of wars were distinguished: (a) wars of defense and expansion, which were basically political and fought because of physical necessity, and to which there were fixed legal limitations (see below); and (b) holy wars, which were compulsory for the entire nation and did not have comparable limitations. This distinction was recognized also in the Second Temple Period (after the return from exile).

This panel from Nineveh (7th cent. BC) depicts Assyrian soldiers pursuing Arabs.

Todd Bolen/www.BiblePlaces.com

Deuteronomy 20 and 21 contain some of the laws of war that were upheld prior to the exile; more laws and practices are found in other sources describing the wars themselves. The laws of war first describe the encouragement of the troops by the priests, who assured them of the support of the Lord (20:1–4). Other sources indicate that the kings and military leaders often assured themselves by consulting oracles; these included the holy ark of the covenant, the ephod, the Urim and Thummim, and various prophets (Jdg. 20:27; 1 Sam. 14:41; 28:6; 30:7–8). The priests and holy ark even accompanied the army on the battlefield in the earlier wars (1 Sam. 4:4; 30:7; 2 Sam. 11:11).

Further, to secure God's aid, the troops would make sacrifices prior to battle (Jdg. 6:20, 26; 20:26)—sometimes even human sacrifices, as in the story of Jephthah's daughter (according to one interpretation of Jdg. 11:39) or of the son of the king of Moab (2 Ki. 3:27). This custom seems also to have been taken from earlier Canaanite traditions, for in many Egyptian reliefs from the late kingdom, depicting the capture of towns in Palestine, the besieged are shown throwing their children from the walls in seeking the gods' favor. Military victory was believed to be the victory of one god over another, often leading to literary depictions of the gods as taking part in actual battles (cf. Josh. 10:11).

The customs and laws of war were fixed and had much in common throughout the ancient Near East. Troops were often drawn from the peasantry, and fighting was generally limited to the agricultural off-seasons—from just after harvest till the first rains. War usually was not "declared"; it was naturally assumed that the strong were free to take possession of the lives and possessions of the weak. Only by keeping a strong army could a nation prevent potential enemies at bay, and the only satisfactory alternative was to accept all of the enemy's demands without going into battle.

Reliefs or wall paintings in Egyptian temples show the conquest of cities in Palestine, with the besieged in the last stages of resistance. These reliefs mainly give details on the methods of Egyptian siege-warfare, which included the use of ladders, mining the walls, and breaching the gates with axes and fire. The battering ram, however, seems not to have been employed by the Egyptians. Most of our information on warfare, however, comes from literary texts, some of which are of the heroic or mythological sort. More realistic war records, prepared by military scribes, enable modern scholars to reconstruct various battles from beginning to end.

The earliest concerns the Battle of Megiddo in the days of Thutmose III. A coalition of many Canaanite kings ("330 rulers") gathered under the leadership of the king of Kadesh on the Orontes and attempted to block the Egyptian army at Megiddo, thus preventing it from penetrating into north Palestine and Syria. The detailed account tells of the deceptive tactics adopted by the Canaanites prior to the battle, to divert the Egyptians toward an ambush. The Egyptian king saw through this ruse and, by a daring march, surprised the Canaanites in their main camp outside the city, defeating them swiftly, though besieged Megiddo held out for seven months longer. The king boasts that he could have captured the city the same day had it not been for his soldiers' desire for loot, which diverted them from pursuing the enemy. This enabled the enemy survivors to reach safety behind the city walls.

Another battle taking place in that period, and about which a complete account survives, is the Battle of Kadesh (1280 BC) between the Egyptian army under Ramses II and the armies of a Syrian (Aramean) league headed by the king of the Hittites. Just as the Canaanites had earlier been fully aware of their military inferiority (especially against the Egyptian archery), so also the Syrians attempted deceit by sending out spies with the intention of their being caught. These gave false information, leading the Egyp-

This relief depicts the conquest of Lachich by Sennacherib's Assyrian army.

tians toward a well-prepared ambush. The ruse seems to have been successful, at least initially, and one of the Egyptian units was wiped out. Egyptian superiority in weaponry and training, and the sudden appearance of a special unit, turned the battle. It is interesting to note that, in both cases, the Egyptians' adversaries avoided open battle, rather seeking the security of strongly fortified cities. The ultimate outcome in either case proved the wisdom of such tactics.

The third battle of which we possess a detailed description took place in the days of Ramses III (c. 1180 BC), in which the Egyptians repulsed the invasion of the "Sea Peoples" (including the Philistines). This battle is depicted on the walls of Ramses' temple at Medinet Habu. The Sea Peoples' attempt was twofold: one wave seems to have come by way of Syria and Palestine, and was defeated near el-'Arish; the second wave came by sea and was defeated in the Nile delta. This is the first detailed description of a sea battle in the history of the ancient Near East. As depicted in the reliefs, the Egyptians won mainly through their superiority in archery—a weapon that their enemies lacked altogether.

Early in the Iron Age (twelfth century BC), political conditions in Palestine changed: the great empires of the previous period, Egypt and the Hittites, were weakened or destroyed, largely by the Sea Peoples; and in the regions between them, many small city-states rose. Palestine was also invaded by two nations new on the political scene and very different in character: the Israelites, who at the time were poorly equipped nomadic tribes settled in the mountainous areas, and groups of Sea Peoples that the Bible collectively calls the "Philistines." These latter settled in the coastal plain and were organized around a pentapolis (Ashdod, Ashkelon, Ekron, Gath, and Gaza); they developed a proper standing army, equipped with iron weapons. Small pockets of the older inhabitants of the land remained; these Canaanites were centered on city-states, with the battle chariot as their most formidable weapon.

Israelite military inferiority forced the tribes also to deception of the enemy; they usually found it too difficult to penetrate fortified cities by force, and thus they resorted to other means, such as by sending spies to seek out hidden ways into the city (Josh. 2). The most interesting biblical story in this connection is the capture of Jericho. Here the army with the priests and the holy ark at its head marched around the city for seven days (6:14–15). At Ai (chs. 8–12), the Israelites succeeded in luring the enemy out of the city by a ruse. Later, David captured Jerusalem by penetrating secretly through an underground water conduit (2 Sam. 5:7–8). Night or dawn attacks were also sprung (1 Sam. 11:11), as well as other forms of surprise attacks (Josh. 10:9). Often armies were split into several parts (usually three) to achieve surprise or to provide a ruse (Jdg. 7:16; cf. also 1 Sam. 11:11; 13:16; 2 Sam. 18:2).

In the period of the settlement, the Israelites had to withstand the attacks of various nomad tribes, especially in the south (the Amalekites) and the Jezreel valley (the Midianites). Warfare against these peoples was conducted in the same manner as before, that is, by means of small and maneuverable units. Larger "militia" units were raised only in times of extreme danger: against the Canaanites (Jdg. 4, 5) or Ammonites (1 Sam. 11), or at a time of intertribal strife (Jdg. 20).

Using these same tactics (combined small attacks and opposing the enemy in open array), the Israelites succeeded, at least at first, in standing up to their bitterest rivals, the

Philistines. It is in this context that we learn of another form of war, that is, the personal duel between two opposing warriors, as in the case of David and Goliath (1 Sam. 17; cf. 2 Sam. 2:12); such a form of fighting is known in other lands. Upon the death of Saul and Jonathan his son, it became obvious that new tactics were called for. The danger presented by the Philistines was the main impetus for the union of the Israelite tribes into a single kingdom to enable successful resistance. Only political unity could bring about a standing well-trained and equipped army.

The army organized by David, under the skilled leadership of Joab, soon enabled the Israelites to achieve the upper hand over the other small states surrounding them. David consolidated the borders of his kingdom and even considerably expanded them. Actually, there was never a day of peace throughout his reign. Most interesting are the detailed chapters describing the wars against the Ammonites and the Arameans (2 Sam. 10:10; 1 Chr. 19), where we learn that Hanun, king of the Ammonites, hired Aramean troops to help him in his defense. Joab soon found himself in the midst of the enemy, and in a very characteristic way he brought in the Israelite militia, which, alongside his small standing army, defeated the Arameans and then turned to besiege the capital of Ammon. The great victories of the Israelite army in the days of David, however, and the expansion into most of Syria (Aram), can be explained only by the fact that by this time the great empires no longer were able to control this region.

After the division of the Israelite nation, the northern and southern kingdoms, at first rivals, came to conduct combined operations against their common enemies, especially the Arameans. Already in the mid-ninth century BC, upon the advent of the mighty armies of Assyria in this region, the petty wars came to an end, and the small states grouped themselves into coalitions so as to be able to stand up to the common foe. From 734 on, Assyria slowly conquered the entire region, taking the petty states one by one. Babylonia, her powerful heir, completed this task.

The Aramean soldiers and their weapons are well known to us from reliefs discovered in various sites. They were fully as strong as the armies of Israel and Judah, and the struggle between them was long-lived. The character of these wars is known from 1 Ki. 20, which contains extensive details. Ben-Hadad king of Damascus, at the head of a league of thirty-two vassal kings, came to Succoth on the eastern bank of the Jordan River, opposite Samaria. When he sent messengers demanding that the Israelites surrender, King Ahab outrightly refused. Ben-Hadad, confident in the superior strength of his forces, ordered them to cross the river and besiege the city of Samaria. The Arameans rather heedlessly began the ascent along the steep path of Wadi Far'ah, the main route from Succoth, well known,

In this relief from Nimrud (8th cent. BC), an Assyrian soldier holds a large shield to protect two archers as they shoot.

ChrisO/Wikimedia Commons

of course, to the Israelites. Rather than waiting for the enemy in Samaria, Ahab gathered his troops (about 700) and ambushed the Arameans while they were still on the march, thoroughly routing them.

This method of ambushing, in narrow mountain defiles by large, well-equipped forces, takes maximum advantage of the difficulties encountered by anyone attempting to penetrate into the hills of Samaria or the Judean mountains; it became one of the standard methods of warfare among the Israelites down to the fall of the kingdoms. A similar battle was conducted between Jehoshaphat king of Judah and a combined Moabite-Ammonite force that was making for Jerusalem through the Judean Desert (2 Chr. 20).

Such a tactic was even more characteristic during the Hellenistic period, when the Jews rose against the Seleucids, and later, during the revolts against Rome. The maneuver is typical of guerrilla warfare and enables small forces to achieve the upper hand over numerically superior armies. Not in vain were the Arameans afraid to enter the mountain passes of Samaria, saying, "Their gods are gods of the hills" (1 Ki. 20:23).

The battles against the Arameans, Moabites, and Ammonites occurred in the open, but not so the wars fought against the mighty armies of Assyria and Babylonia. In the initial clash (in the mid-ninth century), Ahab dared to participate against Assyria in a league of southern Syrian rulers that repulsed the invaders in four successive campaigns, near the city of Qarqar. But a hundred years later, when the Assyrians approached, the petty kingdoms were unable to unite, and the war degenerated into mere defensive actions, centered upon fortified cities, while the Assyrians were in complete control of the countryside.

Assyrian capture of Egyptian fortress.

Todd Bolen/www.BiblePlaces.com

Model of Roman battering ram.
Todd Bolen/www.BiblePlaces.com

Various methods of fighting based on fortified cities are well known from excavations and from Egyptian and Assyrian reliefs, in which this subject was quite popular. Remains of city fortifications, including walls and gates, have been exposed at most of the excavated sites of the Israelite period in Palestine, revealing even minute details. Moreover, systematic study has clarified the development of siege tactics in this period.

The main problem in preparing a city to withstand a siege, besides the construction of the fortifications, was to provide for an adequate source of water within the city walls. This was achieved either by digging vast cisterns for storing quantities of rain water or by diverting water sources beneath the ground to within the fortified area, concealing any original opening outside. Several such water systems have been discovered, mainly dating from the period of the Israelite kingdoms. The famous Siloam tunnel inscription from Jerusalem describes King Hezekiah's efforts to bring water from the Gihon Spring into the city (c. 705 BC). In much later times, extensive water systems were built by Herod the Great to bring huge quantities of water into the same city; similar projects by this king included enormous cisterns constructed at Masada and other fortresses.

The methods of pressing siege were many and varied. We have already noted various ruses employed by the Israelites against Canaanite cities. The Egyptian and Assyrian reliefs reveal even more: scaling walls by means of ladders; breaching walls with battering rams; breaking down gates with axes and fire; and mining beneath walls. Often several methods were employed simultaneously. The Assyrians were depicted as slaying prisoners beneath the very eyes of the besieged so as to weaken their morale.

If a city resisted all these measures, the attackers had to fall back upon the difficult pursuit of an extended siege, cutting off the inhabitants of the city from all supplies and making continuous attacks upon the walls at various locations until a weak spot was found or until the city gave in. After the appearance of the great imperial armies in Palestine, the Israelite kings concentrated their efforts on fortifying and preparing their cities to withstand prolonged sieges. They sometimes succeeded in stemming a siege of many months or even years.

In a relief from Nineveh, there is an exceptional depiction of a Judean city under siege by the Assyrian army; it shows Lachish as the Assyrian troops were storming its walls with many battering rams, light archery in the fore (mostly non-Assyrian troops from vassal kingdoms), then heavy Assyrian spearmen and archers, followed by slingers. The defenders, on their part, attempted to forestall the work of the siege machines by shooting arrows and throwing stones, oil, and flaming torches down upon them.

From the Persian period on, our principal sources are literary. The Greek historians, such as Herodotus, Thucydides, Xenophon, and Diodorus, have provided detailed descriptions of the wars between the Persians and the Greeks, as well as the wars among the Greeks themselves. One of the most interesting of these descriptions, Xenophon's *Anabasis*, tells of the engagement of the Persian army with that of Cyrus, satrap of Sardis, in whose service were the ten thousand Greek mercenaries commanded by Xenophon. In this battle the clear advantage of the new Greek formations over the traditional oriental armies is quite apparent—a superiority that was even more telling in the victorious campaigns of Alexander the Great.

The main force of Greek armies in this period were the units of heavily armed infantry, the *hoplites*. Their name, meaning "heavy-armed," is derived from the large bronze shield they carried into battle on their left arms, protecting most of the body and enabling the warrior to use his right arm for maneuvering his heavy spear, sometimes even at a distance of some ten feet from his enemy. The hoplites also carried a short sword and wore protective armor, including a bronze helmet. These troops fought in a close formation, the phalanx, where the shield of one soldier overlapped that of his neighbor, providing double protection. The superiority of this formation was based upon the fact that the soldiers in the front row, who were in direct contact with the enemy, were immediately supported by their comrades in the rows behind.

From the time of the Peloponnesian wars on, a basic change occurred in the organization of Greek armies. Besides the hoplite,

This panel from Sennacherib's Lachish reliefs depicts Judean exiles leaving the city.
Todd Bolen/www.BiblePlaces.com

This helmet discovered in Persia is dated c. 8th cent. BC.
Z. Radovan/www.BibleLandPictures.com

These bronze scales (9th–7th cent. BC) were used as armor by ancient soldiers.

Mark Borisuk/www.BiblePlaces.com

Statue of Alexander the Great, dated to the 3rd cent. BC.

Giovanni Dall'Orto/ Wikimedia Commons

there was now a lightly armed soldier, the *peltast*, whose name was also derived from a type of shield, smaller and round; these had no protective armor and their principal armament was the small throwing javelin, a weapon derived from Thrace and common especially among mercenaries. In the Macedonian army, the spear was lengthened, sometimes even reaching a length of twenty feet; actually the several rows of the phalanx used spears of varying lengths so as to present the enemy with a maximum of "fire power" at one time. The bow was little used in classical times, but in the Hellenistic period oriental influence brought archers a greater role, and even mounted archers appeared, usually being employed as a protective curtain before the phalanx.

War chariots were not used at all in classical Greece; instead, the Greeks did make use of cavalry as an organic part of the army in several cities. Thus, Athens had cavalry units and, for a short period, also mounted archers. In the classical period, however, the lack of the stirrup seriously impaired the effectiveness of such troops. Alexander, following the lead of his father Philip, made more common use of cavalry, and since then such units held an important place in every battle, especially in outflanking the enemy or pursuing them in flight. The Hellenistic period, too, saw the introduction—again under oriental influence—of heavy cavalry: chariots were also used on a small scale.

As for siege machinery, the Greek sources up to the end of the fifth century

BC are largely silent. We know that only in the beginning of the following century did the Greeks first use a primitive sort of catapult (at Syracuse), which they copied from the Carthaginians. This machine was employed only in siege warfare, throwing darts for a great distance. Later, the catapult was improved, increasing its effective range considerably. Such machines were employed by Alexander in his siege of Tyre (in 332 BC). The Greeks actually had two types of siege machines: the catapult for darts, and the balista for throwing stones; these had an effective range of some six hundred feet, which the Romans later were able to increase to about eight hundred feet.

In the Hellenistic period, the Greeks followed the Persians in using elephants in warfare. Alexander brought over a hundred elephants from India, and Seleucus I had over five hundred. They were particularly effective against enemy cavalry and could also break through the heavy phalanx. In the Battle of Gaza (312 BC), the Egyptian soldiers defended themselves against the Seleucid elephants by studding the battlefield with sharp nails—the first "mine field" in history. Antiochus III employed elephants against the Hasmonean rulers of Judea, leading to the famous story of Eleazar, who was crushed beneath an elephant he had killed with his spear (2 Macc. 13:2). The Romans normally did not use the elephant, probably because of its awkwardness.

The army of the Hasmoneans appears to have been patterned after the Hellenistic model; the later Herodian army, however, was more composite, Hellenistic but with Roman elements. The Roman entry into Palestine in 63 BC brought about a change in the weaponry and in the military formations of this area; actually, it is especially in this field that Roman influence is felt. In excavations of sites in Palestine, few remains of Roman weapons have been found (mainly arrow and javelin heads, a few swords, and scales of armor), though many examples of military architecture are known, such as the siege camps, the circumvallation wall, and the ramp at Masada.

Bronze statue of a Roman soldier.

Todd Bolen/www.BiblePlaces.com

Chapter 6

Religious Life

As the material covered in previous chapters suggests, every aspect of Hebrew society was motivated by religious commitments. The Torah—referring sometimes specifically to the Mosaic law and sometimes more generally to the Pentateuch (Genesis through Deuteronomy), but often most broadly to the Bible's divine instruction as a whole—guided the lives of the Israelites, both as individuals and as a community. In this chapter, however, we consider explicit religious acts and customs, especially in connection with worship.

Altars and High Places

In ancient religious practice generally, the altar took shape from the idea of a raised table of stone or turf on which usually an offering of blood was set before the deity. As early as the time of Noah we find a reference to the building of an altar to God as an expression of thanksgiving and worship (Gen. 8:20). Altars were built also by Abraham, Isaac, and Jacob (Gen. 12:7–8; 13:4, 18; 26:25; 33:20; 35:7). The patriarchs seem to have set up altars as symbols of some notable encounter with God and as memorials of spiritual experience.

An altar in the city of Arad (10th cent. BC).

© Kim Walton

Later among the Hebrews the altar, as an object of ritual and sanctity, became the centerpiece of every sanctuary and the place of sacrifice: "Make an altar of earth for me and sacrifice on it your burnt offerings and fellowship offerings, your sheep and goats and your cattle.... If you make an altar of stones for me, do not build it with dressed stones, for you will defile it if you use a tool on it" (Exod. 20:24–25). This simple structure continued to be a normal Hebrew form throughout the nation's history, allowing individuals the satisfaction of commemorating some act or outcome of private devotion. Joshua built an altar on Mount Ebal (Josh. 8:30), Gideon at Ophra (Jdg. 6:24), Samuel at Ramah (1 Sam. 7:17), Saul at Micmash after his victory there (1 Sam. 14:35), and David on the threshing floor of Araunah (2 Sam. 24:25).

Many types of altars have been discovered in Canaanitish Palestine. They range from the small Early Bronze Age structure of plastered stones set against a wall in a small temple at Ai, to the mud-brick and lime-plastered stone rectangular altars of Middle and Late Bronze Age construction discovered in various sites. A large structure of rubble and unhewn stone at Megiddo, an elevation twenty-six feet in diameter and over four feet high, is perhaps rather to be called a "high place" than an altar.

Some have argued that altars generally were in fact miniature "high places," reflecting the custom of hilltop sacrifice. In any case, the proliferation of altars in pre-Hebrew Palestine demonstrates the manner in which the Mosaic code took over, purified, and adapted to its symbolic ritual and monotheistic purposes the forms and practices of alien religion. It is notable, here and elsewhere, how carefully the Pentateuch regulates the construction and use of the altar. For example, the Hebrew altar was constructed without steps (Exod. 20:26), though Canaanite structures had no such prohibition.

On the other hand, it is true that the OT frequently makes reference to high places, that is, worship sites ordinarily situated on a hill or mountain and commonly associated with false religions. Such sanctuaries could however be found at city gates (cf. 2 Ki. 23:8), which have no apparent connection with an elevated area; and some "high places" were located even in valleys (Jer. 7:31; 19:5–6; 32:35).

The selection of an elevated spot seems psychological, for this location put the worshipper above his immediate environment with its mundane associations and placed him nearer the skies, where the ultimate object of worship was believed to reside. In the plains of ancient Mesopotamia, this interest in height for religious observances led to the construction of the staged or terraced temple tower, or ziggurat. A requirement for the high place was an altar, often simply made of unhewn stones. Related to the high place was a tree or pole of wood that served as an idol or as an adjunct to worship. In Muslim areas, a *weli* (shrine) of a departed sheikh typically has nearby a tree to which the faithful may attach items that will bring the needs of the worshipper to the attention of the spiritual benefactor.

A four-horned altar from Ekron Miqne.

Frequently the high place had a stone symbol, a kind of obelisk or pillar that also was an object of veneration or a commemorative monument. It could also contain images of heathen gods placed in a shrine (cf. 2 Ki. 17:29). Sometimes the high place had a basin or tank where water could be

Remains of the high place in the city of Dan.

Todd Bolen/www.BiblePlaces.com

kept for ablutions or libations. In addition to violating the greatest commandment, the idolatry of the high place might involve the breaking of other divine laws, for the worship of certain deities demanded human sacrifice (usually of infants or children) and the celebration of rites of a sexual nature. Several examples of these high places are known from archaeological evidence.

The Canaanites used the high places long before the Israelite conquest of the land, but the first mention of such a shrine in the Bible appears in connection with that event. The children of Israel were commanded to demolish the high places of the Canaanites, along with the idols of those people (Num. 33:52). At the same time the Lord warned the Israelites that if they disobeyed his laws he would punish them and destroy their high places and false worship (Lev. 26:30; cf. Ps. 78:58). After the destruction of Shiloh and before the building of the temple at Jerusalem, the high place was used as a site of true worship. Samuel blessed the offering that the people made at the high place (1 Sam. 9:12–14). When Saul consulted Samuel, Samuel invited him to take part in the feast at the high place. On his way home, Saul was met by a band of prophets coming down from the high place of Gibeah (1 Sam. 10:5, 10); Saul prophesied with them and also went to the high place (v. 13).

The chronicler remarked that during the reign of David the tabernacle of the Lord was situated at the high place of Gibeon (1 Chr. 16:39; 21:29; 2 Chr. 1:3–4). In the time of

Solomon, mention is made of sacrificing at the high places, because a temple had not yet been built (1 Ki. 3:2–3). At the great high place of Gibeon, he offered a thousand burnt offerings (v. 4; cf. 2 Chr. 1:3–6, 13). In his later years Solomon fell into apostasy and built high places for the Moabite Chemosh and the Ammonite Molech on the mountain east of Jerusalem (1 Ki. 11:7–8; cf. 2 Ki. 23:13).

At the division of the kingdom, Jeroboam tried to prevent the Israelites from going to Jerusalem for the religious festivals: he set up calves of gold at Bethel and Dan (place), built houses on high places, and appointed non-Levitical priests to serve at the high places (1 Ki. 12:26–32; cf. 13:33; 2 Chr. 11:15). A prophet of God predicted that the priests of the high place of Bethel would be sacrificed upon that altar and that the altar would be torn down (1 Ki. 13:2–3). The worship conducted at the high places was one of the sins that would eventually lead to the fall of Samaria, capital of the northern kingdom (2 Ki. 17:7–18).

Meanwhile, in the southern kingdom there was also apostasy; during the reign of Rehoboam, "They also set up for themselves high places, sacred stones and Asherah poles on every high hill and under every spreading tree. There were even male shrine prostitutes in the land" (1 Ki. 14:23–24). When Asa became king of Judah, he initiated many religious reforms, but "he did not remove the high places" (15:12–14). In similar fashion, Jehoshaphat "did what was right in the eyes of the Lord. The high places, however, were not removed, and the people continued to offer sacrifices and burn incense there" (1 Ki. 22:43). His son, the murderous Jehoram, did what was evil and "built high places on the hills of Judah" (2 Chr. 21:11; cf. also 2 Ki. 12:3; 14:3–4; 15:3–4, 34–35; 16:3–4).

The prophets spoke boldly against the high places, whether of Israel or the surrounding nations. Isaiah and Jeremiah mention the high places of Moab (Isa. 15:2; 16:12; Jer. 48:35). Jeremiah refers to the high place of Topheth, which was built in the Hinnom Valley (Jer. 7:31), where people burned their children as offerings to Baal (19:5). Ezekiel and others also prophesied that the high places of Israel would be destroyed (Ezek. 6:3; Hos. 10:8; Amos 7:9). The Babylonian captivity served as a severe lesson to Israel concerning idolatry, and after that event no more is said in the Bible concerning high places.

Tabernacle and Temple

The term *tabernacle*, meaning "tent," is used in the Bible specifically of the sanctuary built under the direction of Moses in the wilderness (the principal passages dealing with it are Exod. 27; 30–31; 35–40; Num. 3:25–38; 4:4–49; 7:1–88). Because God's unique relationship with Israel demanded the undivided worship of the Israelites, it was of supreme importance for a ritual tradition to be established in the wilderness so that Israel could engage in regular spiritual communion with God. The nomadic nature of the sojourn in the Sinai Peninsula precluded the building of a permanent shrine for worship. The only alternative was a portable sanctuary that would embody all that was necessary for the worship of the Lord under nomadic conditions; such a structure could serve also as a prototype of a subsequent permanent building.

Such tent-shrines were by no means unknown in the ancient world. For example, in pre-Islamic times the *qubbah*, a miniature red leather tent with a dome-shaped top, was used for carrying the idols and cultic objects of Arabian tribes. The *qubbahs* were credited with the power of guiding the tribe in its journeys, and in time of war were particularly valuable for the degree of protection they afforded.

At Sinai, Moses was given a divine revelation concerning the nature, construction, and furnishings of the tabernacle (Exod. 25:40). When the task was accomplished, the tent was covered by a cloud and was filled with the divine glory (40:34). Particularly characteristic of its desert origins are the tent curtains, the covering of red leather, and the acacia wood used during the construction.

The tabernacle stood in an outer enclosure or court (Exod. 27:9–18; 38:9–20). Taking the ancient Hebrew cubit to indicate a linear measure of 18 in., the dimensions of the enclosure were 153 ft. in length and 75 ft. in width. The sides were covered with curtains made from finely woven linen. They were about 7 ft. long and were fastened at the top by hooks and at the bottom by silver clasps to sixty supporting pillars of bronze, placed at intervals of some 7 ft. The enclosure thus formed was uninterrupted apart from an opening in the east wall that was screened by linen curtains embroidered in red, purple, and blue. These hangings were about 30 ft. wide, while those at either side of the entrance were a little over 20 ft. wide. The pillars had capitals overlaid with silver and were set in bases of bronze. They were held in position by bronze pins (27:19; 38:20).

Within this open court the various types of sacrificial offerings were presented and the public acts of worship took place. Near the center was situated the great altar of burnt offering made from acacia wood overlaid with bronze (Exod. 27:1–8). This altar measured nearly 8 ft. square and about 5 ft. in height. Its corner projections were known as the "horns" of the altar. The various sacrificial implements associated with

Model of the wilderness tabernacle and the altar.

Todd Bolen/www.BiblePlaces.com

this altar were also made of bronze. A fire that had been miraculously kindled burned continuously on the altar and was tended by the priests (Lev. 6:12; 9:24). Almost in the center of the court was the bronze basin, used by the priests for ritual ablutions (Exod. 30:17–21).

To the western end of the enclosure, parallel to the long walls, stood the tabernacle itself, which was a rectangular structure about 45 x 15 ft. The basic constructional material was acacia wood, easily obtainable in the Sinai Peninsula, fashioned into 48 frames some 15 ft. in height and a little over 2 ft. in width, overlaid with gold (Exod. 26:15–23). The completed tabernacle was divided into two compartments by a curtain on which cherubim (angelic images) were embroidered in red, purple, and blue and which was suspended on four acacia supports. The outermost of these two areas was known as the Holy Place and was about 30 x 15 ft. in area. The innermost part of the tabernacle, the Holy of Holies or the Most Holy Place, was 15 x 15 ft. The entrance to the tabernacle was screened by embroidered curtains supported by five acacia pillars overlaid with gold.

The wooden framework of the tabernacle was adorned by ten linen curtains (Exod. 26:1–7) that were embroidered and decorated with figures of cherubim. It measured about 40 ft. in length and 6 ft. in width, being joined in groups of five to make two large curtains. These were then fastened together by means of loops and golden clasps to form one long curtain 60 ft. long and 42 ft. wide. This was draped over the tabernacle proper in such a way that the embroidery was visible from the inside only through the apertures of the trellis work. Three protective coverings were placed over these curtains. The first was made of goat hair and

The Holy Place in the tabernacle included the table of showbread, also known as the bread of the Presence.

Todd Bolen/www.BiblePlaces.com

measured 45 ft. long and 6 ft. wide; the second consisted of red-dyed rams' hides, while the third was made of fine leather (v. 14).

The information furnished in Exodus makes it difficult to decide whether the tabernacle proper had a flat, somewhat sagging drapery roof or one that was tentlike in shape with a ridgepole and a sloping roof (present-day models of the tabernacle vary in their interpretation). Historically speaking, if the influence of the desert tent was predominant, there may well have been some peak or apex to the structure. If, however, the tabernacle had anything in common with the design of contemporary Phoenician shrines, it probably had a flat roof.

Exodus 25:10–40 describes the furniture of the sanctuary. The Holy Place, or outer chamber of the tabernacle, contained a table for the bread of the Presence ("showbread"), a small acacia-wood structure overlaid with gold. According to Lev. 24:5–9, twelve cakes were placed on this table along with

Model of the ark of the covenant inside the Most Holy Place.

dishes, incense bowls, and pitchers of gold. The bread was renewed each week and was placed in two heaps on the table. Nearby stood the elaborately wrought *menorah* or seven-branched lampstand of pure gold. A carefully executed floral motif was a feature of its design, and associated with the lampstand were gold wick trimmers and trays. The furnishings of the Holy Place were completed by the addition of a small, gold-covered altar of incense. Like the great bronze altar, it had projections on each corner, and like the table of the bread of the Presence, it had golden rings and gold-covered staves so that it could be moved readily.

The furniture of the innermost shrine, the Most Holy Place, consisted only of the ark of the covenant. This was a boxlike structure of acacia wood, whose length was about 4 ft., while its breadth and height were slightly above 2 ft. It was covered on the inside and outside with sheet gold and had golden rings and staves like the table of the bread of the Presence and the altar of incense. The lid of the ark, the "mercy seat," was covered with solid gold. On each end was a golden cherub whose wings stretched toward the center of the lid. The precise appearance of the cherubim is a matter of some uncertainty, but in the OT they were generally represented as winged creatures having feet and hands. Some ivory panels unearthed at Samaria depict a composite figure having a human face, a four-legged animal body, and two elaborate, conspicuous wings.

The ark was the meeting place of God and his people through Moses, and it contained the tablets of the law (Exod. 25:16, 22). According to Heb. 9:4, a pot of manna and Aaron's staff were also placed in the ark. An elaborately worked veil separated the Most Holy Place from the outer compartment of the tabernacle, and when the Israelites journeyed from place to place, the sacred ark was secluded from view by being wrapped in this curtain. Consequently the ark was normally seen only by the high priest, and that on very special ceremonial occasions.

In the tabernacle all the sacrifices and acts of public worship commanded by the law took place. A wealth of detail surrounds the legislation for sacrificial offerings in the Mosaic code, but for practical purposes they could be divided into two groups, animal and vegetable. Flour, cakes, parched corn, and libations of wine for the drink offerings constituted the normal vegetable sacrifices and were frequently offered in conjunction with the thanksgivings made by fire (Lev. 4:10–21; Num. 15:11; 28:7–15). Acceptable animals were unblemished oxen, sheep, and goats, not under eight days old and normally not older than three years (cf. Jdg. 6:25). People who were poor were allowed to offer doves as sacrifices (Exod. 12:5; Lev. 5:7; 9:3–4), but fish were not acceptable. Human sacrifice was explicitly prohibited (Lev. 18:21; 20:25).

Salt, an emblem of purity, was used in conjunction with both the vegetable and animal offerings. The sacrifices were normally presented to the officiating priests in the outer court of the sanctuary, but on occasion they were offered elsewhere (Jdg. 2:5; 1 Sam. 7:17). In all sacrifices it was necessary for the worshipper to present himself in a condition of ritual purity (Exod. 19:14). In animal sacrifices he then identified himself with his offering by laying his hand on it and dedicating it to the purposes of atonement through vicarious sacrifice. Afterward the blood was sprinkled near the altar and the tabernacle proper. When worshippers ate of a sacrifice in the form of a meal, the idea of communion with God was enhanced. On the Day of Atonement the nation's collective sins of inadvertence were forgiven, and on that occasion only the high priest entered the Most Holy Place (Lev. 16).

According to Exod. 40:2 and 17, the tabernacle was set up at Sinai at the beginning of the second year, fourteen days before the Passover celebration of the first anniversary of the exodus. When the structure was dismantled during the wanderings, the ark and the two altars were carried by the Levites who were descendants of Kohath. The remainder of the tabernacle was transported in six covered wagons, each drawn by two oxen (Num. 7:6–9).

During Joshua's lifetime, the tabernacle was settled in Shiloh, in Ephraimite territory, to avoid disputes and jealousy on the part of the tribes. Some think that the fabric of the original tabernacle had become worn out and that it had been replaced by a more substantial building. Later, when

Mt. Hor, where the high priest Aaron died (Num. 20:23–29). The white structure on top is a Muslim mosque.

David wished to institute tabernacle religion in his capital city of Jerusalem, the ark was brought there and lodged in the tent he had pitched for it (2 Sam. 6:12–19). This act climaxed David's plan to give the security and legitimacy of religious sanction to his newly established monarchy.

David himself, to be sure, thought it was inappropriate for him to live in a fine "house of cedar, while the ark of God remains in a tent" (2 Sam. 7:2), and so he proposed to build a temple. This goal, however, was not fulfilled until the accession of Solomon to the throne (7:12–13). David did prepare for it, however, both in plans and materials (1 Chr. 22:1–19; 28:1–29:9) and more especially by arranging its liturgical service (23:1–26:19).

There are no known remains of Solomon's temple. It clearly was patterned after the tabernacle, but was much more complex and ornate. The Phoenicians, who were more advanced culturally than the Hebrews, played a great part in the design and construction of the temple. Archaeologists have discovered remains in Phoenicia and Syria that have increased our understanding of the details and motifs of the temple of Jerusalem. Especially useful is the temple found at Tell Tainat in Syria, which was built at about the same time as Solomon's. Its architectural details are believed to be the best guide extant today in reconstructing the details of Solomon's temple, which was noted for lavish beauty of detail rather than for great size.

Seven years were required to complete the temple. It was dedicated in Solomon's eleventh year, c. 950 BC (1 Ki. 6:38), and was destroyed when the Babylonians burned Jerusalem in 586. The temple was in some respects a prefabricated building. It was made of limestone finished at the quarries (6:7) in or near Jerusalem. When the stones

Reconstruction of the Jerusalem temple in NT times.

Ariely/Wikimedia Commons

Reconstruction of the Tower of Antonia, on the NW corner of the temple mount.

Berthold Werner/Wikimedia Commons

were brought to the building site, they were built into the wall according to plan. The stone walls were covered with paneling of Lebanese cedar wood, probably finished by skilled Phoenician craftsmen (5:6; 6:15, 18).

The temple consisted of three sections: (a) the porch or portico, through which the temple proper was entered (1 Ki. 6:3); (b) the Holy Place, a nave that was 30 ft. wide, 60 long, and 45 high, lighted by clerestory windows (vv. 3–4); it was paneled with cedar, with gold inlay to relieve the wooden monotony and to add grandeur; (c) the Most Holy Place or "inner sanctuary," a 30-ft. cube, windowless and overlaid with gold (v. 5; 2 Chr. 3:8–13). It had a raised floor, and the cubicle was reached by steps from the Holy Place. Here God especially manifested his presence by the glory cloud.

The structure was built on a high platform that was reached by ten steps, a dramatic approach for religious processions. On this platform, before the entrance to the portico, stood two pillars, called Jakin and Boaz (1 Ki. 7:15–22). Just behind them, doors led to the portico, a kind of antechamber to the Holy Place. The cypress doors were carved with cherubim, palm trees, and open flowers inlaid with gold (6:18, 32, 35).

At both sides and at the rear of the temple were built three-storied rooms. They were not as high as the central structure, and thus the light from the clerestory windows supplied illumination for the Holy Place. This clerestory feature was perhaps an ancestor of the same window arrangement of the medieval cathedrals (recessed window-walls rising above the lower wings or aisle portions). In the chambers around the sanctuary the immense temple treasury was kept (1 Ki. 7:51).

In the courtyard in front of the temple stood the altar of burnt offering, the central

The double-arched Golden Gate, which originally led to the temple mount in Jerusalem.

www.HolyLandPhotos.org

The Arch of Titus in Rome includes a depiction of treasures from the Jerusalem temple, such as the seven-branched lampstand or menorah, being carried in triumphal procession.

Gunnar Bach Pedersen/Wikimedia Commons

object in the sacrificial service. It was made of brass (2 Chr. 4:1) and probably stood on the great rock that is today covered by the Dome of the Rock on the Ḥaram esh-Sharif. South of the altar stood the copper alloy basin or molten sea (1 Ki. 7:23–26). This mammoth cast "sea" was made in the Jordan Valley, where clay suitable for molding the metal was to be found. It was 3.5 in. thick, about 15 ft. in diameter, and 7.5 ft. high, and stood on the backs of twelve bulls, three facing in each direction.

Priests and Levites

Among the Israelite tribes descended from the sons of Jacob, that of Levi was considered the priestly tribe, but only the descendants of Aaron functioned as priests in a strict sense. The other "Levites" (i.e., descendants of Levi) had a variety of religious duties, and thus the term *Levite* came to signify something like "priestly attendant."

In the pagan countries surrounding Israel, such as Egypt and Babylon, priesthood was closely connected with magic and superstition. Numerous examples are available to illustrate the firm tie between the priesthood and the occult in ancient religions. The priesthood in Israel, however, takes into account another dimension in the religious world, that of supernatural revelation.

The priesthood represented the nation's relationship with God. The covenant of God was mediated through the priests (Mal. 2:4–6; cf. Num. 18:19; Jer. 33:20–26). Fundamentally, however, the entire nation was intended to be a kingdom of priests and a holy people (Exod. 19:5–6; cf. Lev. 11:44–45; Num. 15:40; Isa. 61:6). The fact that God vested priestly functions in one tribe did not release the rest of the nation from their original obligation.

When the priests ministered, they did so as the representatives of the people. It was a practical necessity that the corporate obligation of the covenant people should be carried out by priestly representatives. Furthermore, the priests in their separated condition symbolized the purity and holiness God required. They were a visible reminder of God's righteous requirements. The primary function of the Levitical priesthood, therefore, was to maintain and assure the holiness of the chosen people of God (Exod. 28:38; Lev. 10:7; Num. 18:1).

The priests were guardians of the sanctuary, and much of their time was occupied with cultic responsibilities, especially the offering of sacrifices. Another important function was to discover the will of God by means of the ephod (1 Sam. 23:6–12) and more generally to give instruction in the law (cf. Mal. 2). In addition, the priest acted as judge, a consequence of his imparting answers to legal questions (2 Chr. 19:8).

The priesthood was divided into three groups. (a) The lowest order of priesthood consisted of the Levites, who cared for the service of the sanctuary. (b) Aaron and his descendants, who were set apart for the special office of priest, were above the Levites. Only they could minister at the sacrifices of the altar. (c) The highest level of the priesthood was the high priest, and Aaron was the first to occupy that position. The high priest represented the purity of the priesthood. He bore the names of all the tribes of Israel on his breastpiece into the sanctuary, thus representing all the people before God (Exod. 28:29). Only he could enter the holiest of all, and only on one day a year, to make expiation for the sins of the entire nation. During the reigns of David and especially

The inscription on this stone means "place of trumpeting"; it was the platform from which the temple priests would blow the trumpet.

Todd Bolen/www.BiblePlaces.com

Remains of a synagogue at Capernaum, dated to the 4th–5th cent. AD.

Solomon, Zadok son of Ahitub rose to such prominence that subsequent high priests were chosen only from the Zadokite line. Later, during the intertestamental period, the legitimacy of the Zadokite priesthood played a major role in politics and religion.

The ceremonies connected with the consecration of the priests are described in Exod. 29 and Lev. 8. They included a ritual bathing, anointing, clothing, and sacrifices. The washing was intended to symbolize cleansing of heart for the duties that were so intimately related to the purity of the nation before God. The anointing (Lev. 8:10–11) involved pouring of oil on the head of the high priest and the sprinkling of oil on the garments of the other priests (vv. 22–24). The vestments of the priests, and especially of the high priest, were both costly and beautiful (Exod. 28:3–5; Lev. 8:7–9). The consecration sacrifices included a sin offering (8:14–17), burnt offering (vv. 18–21), and a special consecration offering (vv. 22–32). Ram's blood was applied to the right ear, thumb, and toe of Aaron and his sons to symbolize complete bodily consecration to the Lord.

Feasts

Sacred festivals held an important place in Jewish religion. They were religious services accompanied by demonstrations of joy and gladness. In Lev. 23, where they are described most fully, they are called "sacred assemblies" (KJV, "holy convocations"). Their times were fixed by divine appointment. Their purpose was to promote spiritual interests of the community. The people met in holy fellowship for acts and purposes of sacred worship. They met before God in holy assemblies.

The weekly *Sabbath* (Lev. 23:3). This celebration stood at the head of the sacred seasons. The holy meetings by which the Sabbath was distinguished were quite local. Families and other small groups assembled under the guidance of Levites or elders and engaged in common acts of devotion, the forms and manner of which were not prescribed. Little is known of where or how the people met before the captivity, but after it they met in synagogues and were led in worship by teachers learned in the law.

The *Passover* (Lev. 23:4–8). This celebration was the first of all the annual feasts, and historically and religiously it was the most important of all. It was called both the Feast of the Passover and the Feast of Unleavened Bread, the two really forming a double festival. It was celebrated on the first month of the religious year, on the fourteenth of Nisan (corresponding to March–April), and commemorated the deliverance of the Jews from Egypt and the establishment of Israel as a nation by God's redemptive act. The Lord had entered Egypt bent on judgment but, seeing the blood on the doorpost of the Israelite houses, he "passed over" them, completely at peace with those who were sheltering there (Exod. 12:12–13). This combined feast was one of the three that all male Jews who were physically able and ceremonially clean were required by the Mosaic law to attend (Exod. 23:17; Deut. 16:16). The other two were the Feast of Weeks, or Pentecost, and the Feast of Tabernacles. These were known as the pilgrimage festivals; on all of them special sacrifices were offered, varying according to the character of the festival (Num. 28–29).

The *Feast of Pentecost* (Lev. 23:15–21). Other names for Pentecost are the Feast of Weeks, the Day of the Firstfruits, and the Feast of Harvests. It was celebrated on the sixth day of the month of Sivan (May–June), seven weeks after the offering of the wave sheaf after the Passover. The later name *Pentecost* (from a Gk. word meaning "fiftieth") originated from the fact that there was an interval of fifty days between the two feasts. This festival lasted a single day (Deut. 16:9–12) and marked the completion of the wheat harvest. Its characteristic ritual was the offering and waving of two loaves of leavened bread, made from ripe grain that had just been harvested. This was done by the priest in the name of the congregation. In addition to these wave offerings, the people were to give to the Lord an offering of the firstfruits of their produce. The amount of the offering was not designated.

The *Feast of Trumpets or New Moon* (Lev. 23:23–25). This celebration was held on the first day of the seventh month, Tishri (Sept.–Oct.), which began the civil year of the Jews. It corresponded to our New Year's Day, and on it, from morning to evening, horns and trumpets were blown. After the exile the day was observed by the public reading of the law and by general rejoicing.

The *Day of Atonement* (Lev. 23:26–32). This sacred event (*Yom Kippur*) was observed on the tenth day of Tishri. It was really less a feast than a fast, as the distinctive character and purpose of the day was to bring the collective sin of the whole year to remembrance so that it might earnestly be dealt with and atoned for. On this day the high priest made confession of all the sins of the community and entered on their behalf into the Most Holy Place with the blood of reconciliation. It was a solemn occasion, when God's people through godly sorrow and atonement for sin entered into the rest of God's mercy and favor. In receiving his forgiveness, they

The Jewish Sacred Year

Month		*Special Days*
Nisan	(March-April)	14—Passover 15—Unleavened Bread 21—Close of Passover
Iyar	(April-May)	
Sivan	(May-June)	6—Feast of Pentecost—seven weeks after the Passover (Anniversary of the giving of the law on Mt. Sinai)
Tammuz	(June-July)	
Ab	(July-August)	
Elul	(August-September)	
Tishri	(September-October)	1 & 2—Feast of Trumpets Rosh Hashanah, beginning of the civil year 10—Day of Atonement 15-21—Feast of Tabernacles
Marheshvan	(October-November)	25—Feast of Lights, Dedication, Hanukkah
Kislev	(November-December)	
Tebeth	(December-January)	
Shebat	(January-February)	
Adar	(February-March)	14—Feast of Purim

could rejoice before him and carry out his commandments.

The *Feast of Tabernacles* (Lev. 23:33–43). Also called the Feast of Booths or Ingathering, this was the last of the sacred festivals under the old covenant in preexilic times. It began five days after the Day of Atonement (Lev. 23:34; Deut. 16:13) and lasted seven days. It marked the completion of the harvest and historically commemorated the wanderings in the wilderness. During this festival people lived in booths and tents to remind themselves of how their forefathers wandered in the wilderness and lived in booths. The sacrifices were more numerous than those during the other festivals. The last day of the feast marked the conclusion of the ecclesiastical year. The whole celebration was popular and joyous in nature.

Besides the above feasts, which were all preexilic and instituted by God, the Jews after the captivity added two others, the Feast of Lights (Hanukkah, i.e., Dedication) and the Feast of Purim.

Sacrifices and Offerings

A sacrifice is an act of worship in which offering is made to God of some material object belonging to the offerer; this offering is consumed in the ceremony in order to attain, restore, maintain, or celebrate fellowship with God. The first record of such an act is found in Gen. 4:3–5, which states that "Cain brought some of the fruits of the soil as an offering to the LORD. But Abel …

brought ... fat portions from some of the firstborn of his flock. The Lord looked with favor on Abel and his offering, but on Cain and his offering he did not look with favor." Some believe that God found Abel's offering acceptable because it involved a bloody sacrifice; others argue that the reason was Abel's motive and attitude (cf. Heb. 11:4).

The sacrifice of Noah after the flood (Gen. 8:20–21) is called a burnt offering and is closely connected with the covenant of God (9:8–17). In the sacrifices of Abraham, several of which are mentioned (12:7–8; 13:4, 18; 15:9–10), he acted as his own priest and made offerings to express his adoration of God and probably to atone for sin. The patriarchs Isaac and Jacob regularly offered sacrifices (26:25; 28:18; 31:54; 33:20; 35:7; 46:1; cf. also Job 1:5; 42:7–9). The Israelites during their sojourn in Egypt no doubt were accustomed to animal sacrifices. It was to some such feast that Moses asked the pharaoh for permission to go into the wilderness (Exod. 3:18; 5:3; 7:16); and he requested herds and flocks for the feast to offer burnt offerings and sacrifices (10:24–25). The sacrifice of the Passover (12:3–11) brings out forcibly the idea of salvation from death.

The establishment of the covenant between Israel and the Lord was accompanied by solemn sacrifices. The foundational principle of this covenant was *obedience*, not sacrifices (Exod. 19:4–8). Sacrifices were important—aids to obedience, but valueless without it. After the division of the kingdom in 931 BC, calf worship was established

A *sukkah* or booth such as would have been used to celebrate the Feast of Tabernacles.

Kim Guess/www.BiblePlaces.com

at Dan and Bethel, with priests, altars, and ritual (1 Ki. 12:27–28). High places, most of them very corrupt, were in use in both kingdoms until the time of the exile, although occasionally attempts were made in the southern kingdom to remove them. With the destruction of the temple in Jerusalem in 586 BC the entire cultus was suspended, but on the return from the captivity an altar was built and sacrifices resumed. Sacrifices were made in the temple in Jerusalem until its destruction by the Romans in AD 70. The Jews have offered none since then.

The Bible makes clear that every offering had to be the honestly acquired property of the offerer (2 Sam. 24:24). Sacrifices had value in the eyes of the Lord only when they were made in acknowledgment of his sovereign majesty, expressed in obedience to him, and with a sincere desire to enjoy his favor. The only animals allowed for sacrifice were oxen, sheep, goats, and pigeons (wild animals and fish could not be offered). The produce of the field allowed for offerings was wine, oil, or grain (either in the ear or in the form of meal, dough, or cakes).

Both male and female animals were accepted for sacrifice, although for some sacrifices the male was prescribed. With one exception (Lev. 22:23), no animal with any sort of wound or defect could be offered (22:21–24). The law commanded that animals be at least eight days old (22:27); and in some cases the age of the animal is specified (9:3; 12:6; Num. 28:3, 9, 11). According to the later rabbis, animals more than three years old could not be sacrificed. There was no prescription of age or sex with regard

Goats were among the animals that could be offered as sacrifices in Hebrew worship.

to pigeons or turtledoves, but they were offered only by the poor as substitutes for other animals.

The *sin offering* was required for (a) sins unconsciously or unintentionally committed; (b) sins committed intentionally, but with mitigating circumstances; (c) certain kinds of ceremonial defilements; and (d) sins deliberately committed but afterward voluntarily confessed (Lev. 4:1–5:13; 6:24–30; 12:6–8). For conscious and deliberate violations of the law no atonement was possible, though in some instances provision was made in the guilt offerings. Sin offerings were made for the whole congregation on all the feast days and especially on the Day of Atonement. They were also offered on the occasion of the consecration of priests and Levites (Exod. 29:10–14, 36). Every year, on the great Day of Atonement, sin offerings were brought for the high priest. With the exception of these important national occasions, the sin offerings were presented only when special circumstances demanded expiation of sin.

The costliness of the offering and the procedure to be followed depended on the offender. For the high priest a young bullock was the appointed offering (Lev. 4:3); for a prince it was a male goat (4:22–23); in ordinary cases a female goat or a sheep was sufficient. The poor could offer two pigeons, and where even these were too much, a small portion of fine flour was substituted (5:7, 11).

In all other blood sacrifices the blood was simply poured around the altar; in this one the blood was sprinkled. If a member of the congregation made the offering, the blood was smeared on the horns of the altar in the forecourt (Lev. 4:7, 18, 25, 30). When a sin offering was for a priest or the whole congregation, the officiating priest took some of the blood of the sacrifice into the Holy Place and sprinkled it seven times before the veil of the sanctuary and then smeared it on the horns of the altar of incense. The blood that was left had to be poured out at the base of the altar. After the blood was sprinkled, the fat portions of the animal were burned on the altar. The remainder of the flesh was disposed of in two ways: in the case of sin offerings of any of the congregation the flesh was eaten in the forecourt by the officiating priest and his sons; in the case of sin offerings for a priest or for the whole congregation, the whole animal was burned outside the camp in a clean place.

The *guilt offering* (KJV, "trespass offering") was a special kind of sin offering for transgressions where restitution or other legal satisfaction could be made or was made (Lev. 5:14–6:7). When the rights of God or neighbor were violated, the wrong had to be righted, the broken law honored, and the sin expiated by a guilt offering. The offering, which was almost always a lamb (with only one exception, 14:12), was given after the required satisfaction had been made. The ritual was the same as in the sin offering, except that the blood was not sprinkled but poured over the surface of the altar. Its main purpose was to make expiation for withholding that which was due either to God (like neglect to pay at the proper time what was required at the sanctuary) or to people (robbery, failure to return a deposit, etc.). The sin offering of a lamb made atonement to God. Restitution, with an additional one-fifth, made reparation to human beings.

The *burnt offering* (Lev. 1) was distinctive in that it was wholly consumed on the altar, while in other animal sacrifices only the fat portions were burned. The purpose of the offering was propitiation (divine appeasement), but with this idea was united

The Canaanite temple complex in Megiddo included a round altar for sacrifices.
Hanay/Wikimedia Commons

another: the entire consecration of the worshipper to the Lord. Because of the regularity and frequency with which it was offered, it was called the "continual burnt offering" (Exod. 29:42 NASB); and because no part was left for human consumption, it was also called the "whole burnt offering" (Ps. 51:19 NASB). This was the normal sacrifice of the Israelite in proper covenant relationship with God and was the only sacrifice regularly appointed for the sanctuary service. It was offered every day, in the morning and in the evening. On ordinary days a yearling lamb was sacrificed; on the Sabbath day two lambs were offered at morning and evening sacrifice (Num. 28:9–10). On other special feast days a larger number of animals was offered. There were also private burnt offerings specified in other situations (see Num. 6; Exod. 29:15; Lev. 12:6; 14:9; 15:15, 30). The burnt offering was the only sacrifice that a non-Israelite was permitted to bring (17:8; 22:18, 25).

The *fellowship offering* (Lev. 3; KJV, "peace offering"; NRSV, "sacrifice of well-being") was not commanded to be offered at any set time except Pentecost (23:20); it was presented spontaneously as the feelings of the worshipper prompted (19:5). The ritual was the same as for the sin offering, except that the blood was wholly poured on the altar, as in the guilt offering and burnt offering. The fat was burned; the breast and thigh were kept by the priests; and the rest of the flesh was eaten at the sanctuary by the sacrificer and his friends (Lev. 7:15–16, 30–34; Deut. 12:1, 17–18). A meat and drink offering always accompanied this sacrifice. This meal denoted the fellowship that existed between the worshipper and God and was a symbol and pledge of friendship and peace with him. There were three kinds of fellowship offerings: praise offerings, votive offerings, and freewill offerings. For all three classes oxen, sheep, and goats of either sex could be offered (Lev. 3:1, 6, 12). The animals had to be without blemish, except for the freewill offerings, where animals with too short or too long a limb were allowed (22:23). Fellowship offerings were presented also on occasions of great public solemnity or rejoicing.

In addition, there were two kinds of "vegetable" or bloodless offerings. The *grain offerings* consisted of fine flour or of unleavened bread, cakes, wafers, or of ears of grain toasted, always with salt and with olive oil (Lev. 2:1–16; 6:14–18). They were sometimes accompanied by frankincense. Only a portion was consumed by fire on the altar; the rest was kept by the priests, who ate it in a holy place (6:16; 10:12–13). The grain offering accompanied the other offerings, except the sin offering, on all important occasions (7:11–14; Num. 15). It always followed the morning and evening burnt offerings. The *drink offerings* were made only in connection with the grain offering that accompanied all burnt offerings and all fellowship offerings that were Nazirite, votive, or freewill (Num. 6:17; 15:1–2). The drink offering consisted of wine, which was poured out on the altar, probably on the flesh of the sacrifice.

Ritual Purity

In many societies the concept of *tabu* (or *taboo*) has played an important role. *Tabu* is a word of Polynesian origin and means "forbidden" or "excluded" (*tambu, tapu*). A related concept is *mana*, which refers to the more friendly powers behind the universe. In order to cope with persons or objects under *tabu*, incantations and rites are performed. In this manner primitive human beings tried to cope with intruding spirits and neutralize their effect. All unseen powers constituted a threat that could be dealt with only by the application of magic.

Some have argued that the Levitical concepts of clean and unclean are only variations of the primitive notion of *tabu*. Biblical statements about ritual purity, however, are always related to Israel's God, who is never conceived as a merely numinous force. Cultic cleanness derives from a sense of God's holy presence and aims at uncompromising and complete separation from idol worship (cf. Lev. 15:31). Moreover, the Levitical requirements are never far removed from the demand for moral rectitude (cf. 19:9–18).

The Hebrew terms for "clean" and "unclean" are seldom related to mere questions of hygiene, but are mainly religious concepts. As such the principle of cleanness affects almost every aspect of life, for the dichotomy between spiritual and material is foreign to the Bible. The Scriptures move in a totally religious culture that covers life in its entirety. Indeed, the so-called Code of Holiness (Lev. 17–26) and comparable passages attach the concepts of cleanness and uncleanness to persons, animals, and inanimate objects alike.

Persons. Impurity is contracted mainly by physical contact. Everything unclean conveys impurity to that which touches it: a dead body (Lev. 21:1; cf. 5:2; Num. 9:6–10; 19:1–2, 13; 31:19); a "crawling thing" (Lev. 22:5); the carcass of an animal, particularly that of the pig (Lev. 11:28; cf. Deut. 14:8); a menstruous woman (Lev. 15:19); a woman in childbirth (12:4–5). Priests are especially susceptible, for uncleanness would prevent them from acceptably performing their sacred functions (21:11; cf. Hag. 2:13).

Leprosy (referring to various skin diseases) was regarded as a most serious cause of pollution, not only because of the physical deadliness involved, but also because it was considered a mark of divine disfavor. For this reason the purificatory rites for this disease required additional sin offerings and burnt offerings (Lev. 14:13). Levitical impurity could also be contracted from one's own person, as in the case of nocturnal emission of semen (15:16; cf. Deut. 23:10). Uncleanness in a more numinous sense was contracted by contact with hallowed things, such as the ashes of the red heifer, and therefore it required purificatory rites (Num. 19:7–8).

Animals. Some animals were regarded in pagan circles as sacred: fish, for example, was *tabu* in Egypt and Syria; pigs were con-

These stone vessels from NT times may have been used to insure the purity of the products stored in them.
Z. Radovan/www.BibleLandPictures.com

sidered holy animals in Crete and Babylon. In the Pentateuch, however, the codes dealing with clean and unclean animals were intended to distinguish Israel from the surrounding nations (cf. Lev. 20:23). The differentiation between animals allowed and prohibited for consumption was established on the following principles: (a) Hygiene: all scavengers and birds of prey were prohibited, since they fed upon rotting carrion. (b) Idolatry: animals used in pagan cults or associated with witchcraft were automatically excluded; these included swine, dogs, mice, serpents, hares, insects like beetles, etc. (c) Repulsion: these animals are sometimes described as "swarming" (11:41; NIV, "that moves about on the ground") and were prohibited probably for aesthetic reasons. (4) Local custom: exotic or unknown animals were felt to be strange and therefore unclean.

The law lays down rules for distinguishing between allowed and disallowed animals: whatever has a split hoof and chews the cud may be eaten (Lev. 11:3; Deut. 14:3–8). All other animals are forbidden even though they may fulfill part of the requirements. In regard to fish, fins and scales were both necessary: any creature lacking either of these was an abomination (Lev. 11:9–10). The law prohibited eating winged creatures that were quadrupeds, but six-legged locusts, crickets, and grasshoppers were allowed (11:20–23). In some way these prohibitions were connected to the command against the eating of blood (cf. 3:17; 17:10–14; Deut. 12:16, 23–25; 15:23) and possibly the pagan practice of tearing a limb from a living animal as a result of religious frenzy.

Objects. The qualities of cleanness and uncleanness applied to objects as well as to persons and animals. Objects might contract uncleanness by contact with an unclean source, whether human or animal. In the case of "leprosy," houses and walls seemed to be credited with the disease on their own accord (cf. Lev. 14:34–53; the NIV therefore translates "spreading mildew" rather than "leprosy").

Those who were ceremonially unclean transmitted their condition to everything they touched: seat, bed, saddle, garments, earthen vessels, etc. Anyone touching these objects acquired uncleanness to a secondary degree. First-degree uncleanness required purificatory rites lasting seven days (Lev. 15:13), whereas secondary uncleanness lasted only till the evening and was removed by washing (15:6–7). Cultic objects were also liable to uncleanness and required cleansing. Atonement was to be made for the holy place (16:16, 20), for the altar (vv. 18–19), for the mercy seat (v. 15), and for the veil of the sanctuary (4:6). Purificatory rites were also required for those who handled the ashes of the heifer (Num. 19:10) and the water for impurity (v. 20).

The priestly cultus evolved a complicated system of purificatory rites. Careful provision is made for every form of pollution both cultic and moral. It is based upon the principle that uncleanness is the cause of separation from God who is holy. To remove the offense and restore the relationship expiatory rites are prescribed. These rites take the form of cathartic ceremonies through various means, as follows:

(a) *Water* is a natural means of cleansing and is widely used in religious cults. The law refers to the water of expiation (Num. 8:7), the water of purification (19:9, 13, et al.), and running water (literally, "living water," cf. 19:17). In all rites of cleansing, water plays an important part (e.g., Lev. 6:28; 8:6; 14:8–9, 51–52; cf. Ezek. 36:25).

(b) The purpose of the cult was to provide expiation. This required the shedding of *sacrificial blood* (cf. Heb. 9:22). The altar sacrifices served a cathartic purpose to restore by purification the broken relationship between the worshipper and God. Aaron and his sons were anointed to the priesthood with sacrificial blood (Lev. 8:23–24). Such blood was used also for the cleansing of leprosy (14:4–5); similarly the blood of the sin offering accomplished atonement (16:11–19).

(c) To the *ashes* of the sacrificial victim were ascribed purging properties (Num. 19:17). This was especially so in the case of the red heifer, which was used exclusively for purificatory purposes (19:1–13).

(d) Together with scarlet and hyssop, *cedarwood* was prescribed as a means of purification (Lev. 14:4, 5, 51–52). Hyssop is an herb that was credited with special cathartic potency as a means of sprinkling holy water (cf. Ps. 51:7).

(e) The most radical means of purification was *fire*. Metal vessels were purged in this way (Num. 31:22–23). To prevent pollution the remains of the paschal sacrifice were ordered to be burned (Exod. 12:10). Other sacrifices were treated in the same manner (Lev. 7:17). The sin offering was totally burned, and then the ashes had to be removed from the camp (Lev. 4:12). In extreme cases of moral lapse such as incest, punishment of persons was by burning (20:14; 21:9); yet this can hardly be regarded as remedial purification. Idols were to be destroyed by burning. This Moses did with the golden calf in the wilderness (Exod. 32:20; Deut. 9:21). A city that became idolatrous was to be razed and burnt by fire with everything in it (13:12–16). It was never to be rebuilt.

The NT refers to the Jewish rites of purification in several passages. After the birth of Jesus, he was brought to the temple for the purificatory rites (Lk. 2:22; cf. Exod. 13:2, 13; Lev. 12:2–8). The disciples of John the Baptist and the Jews discussed matters concerning purification (Jn. 3:25). At the wedding at Cana there were jars "for the Jewish rites of purification" (2:6 NRSV). The healed lepers were sent to appear before the priests to offer the sacrifice for their cleansing as commanded by Moses (Mk. 1:44; Lk. 5:14; cf. Lev. 13:49; 14:2–32).

In the teaching of Jesus and his apostles, however, the contrast between clean and unclean is freed from the cultic aspects. The emphasis is upon inward purity. The pure in heart who see God (Matt. 5:8) are those who have received forgiveness and grace through faith in Jesus Christ. In the controversies between Jesus and the Pharisees, the question of ceremonial cleanness plays an important role, because the rabbis defined in great detail the circumstances causing ceremonial impurity. Such concerns could lead to the neglect of "the more important matters" (Matt. 23:23). Jesus accused the Pharisees of being so concerned with the outside of cups and plates that they overlooked what was inside, namely, extortion and rapacity (23:25–26). He demanded that the cleansing process start from within (Lk. 11:41). By the "inside" Jesus means the heart (cf. Mk. 7:14–23). The same issue recurs in the matter of the washing of hands (7:2–8).

A key passage is Acts 10:11–14 (TNIV), which relates a vision Peter had: "He saw heaven opened and something like a large sheet being let down to earth by its four corners. It contained all kinds of four-footed animals, as well as reptiles and birds. Then a voice told him, 'Get up, Peter. Kill and eat.' 'Surely not, Lord!' Peter replied. 'I have never eaten anything impure or unclean.'" This interchange, repeated a second and a third time, was meant to prepare Peter to preach the gospel to Gentiles, who were regarded as unclean by the Jews (cf. 10:28). Later the elders and apostles in Jerusalem recognized non-Jewish believers could be received into the church without requiring them to submit to the ceremonial laws (see Acts 15).

Synagogue

The term *synagogue* refers to a Jewish house of worship—but distinct from the Jerusalem temple—or to the congregation that meets in such a place. Some writers and rabbis traced this institution back to Moses, but this tradition has no historical basis. It is likely that the synagogue had its precursor during the Babylonian exile in the spontaneous gatherings of the Jewish people on the Sabbath and also on special feast days. Since religion stood at the very center of Jewish existence, these gatherings naturally took on a religious significance. Without access to the temple and its rituals, the Jews of the exile needed mutual encouragement in the faithful practice of their religion and in the hope of a restoration to the land. These they sought and found in spontaneous assemblies, which proved to be of such religious value that they quickly spread throughout the lands of the Diaspora (dispersion or scattering).

From about the second century BC onward, the sect of the Pharisees assumed a leading role in the synagogues. It was an institution peculiarly adapted to achieve their ends. By NT times the synagogue was a firmly established institution among the Jews, who considered it to be an ancient institution, as the words of James in Acts 15:21 (TNIV) show: "For the law of Moses has been preached in every city from the earliest times and is read in the synagogues

Reconstruction of the synagogue at Korazin (2nd–3rd cent. AD).

on every Sabbath." Synagogues could have been found everywhere in the Hellenistic world where there were sufficient Jews to maintain one. In large Jewish centers there would have been many.

The chief purpose of the synagogue was not primarily public worship, but instruction in the Holy Scriptures. The very nature of Judaism, a religion of revelation, demanded such an institution to survive. All of the rabbis emphasized the importance of knowing the law, and regular attendance at the synagogue met this educational need.

Every synagogue had at least two officials. (a) The ruler of the synagogue was probably elected by the elders of the congregation. He was responsible for the building and property; the general oversight of the public worship, including the maintenance of order (cf. Lk. 13:14); the appointing of persons to read the Scriptures and to pray; and the inviting of strangers to address the congregation. Generally there was only one ruler for each synagogue, but some synagogues had more (Acts 13:15).

(b) The *hazan* or attendant was a paid officer whose special duty was the care of the synagogue building and its furniture, in particular the rolls of Scripture. During the worship it was the hazan who brought forth the roll from the chest and handed it to the appointed reader. He also returned it to its proper place at the conclusion of the reading (Lk. 4:20). He had numerous other duties, which included the instruction of children in reading, the administration of scourgings, and the blowing of three blasts on the trumpet from the roof of the synagogue to announce the beginning and end of the Sabbath. Since his work was closely associated with the synagogue building and its equipment, he sometimes lived under its roof.

Synagogue buildings varied greatly. They were usually built of stone and lay north and south, with the entrance at the south end. Their size and elegance were largely determined by the numerical strength and prosperity of the Jewish communities in which they were built. The principal items of furniture were (a) a chest in which the rolls of Scripture were kept, wrapped in linen cloth; (b) a platform or elevated place on which a reading desk stood; (c) lamps and candelabra, trombones and trumpets; and (d) benches on which the worshippers sat.

The congregation was separated, the men on one side and the women on the other. The more prominent members took the front seats. The service began with the recitation of the Jewish confession of faith, known as the *Shema*: "Hear, O Israel: The LORD our God, the LORD is one. Love the LORD your God with all your heart and with all your soul and with all your strength" (Deut. 6:4–5). This was both preceded and followed by thanksgivings, one of which reads: "Blessed art thou, O Lord our God, King of the world, maker of light and creator of darkness, author of peace and creator of all things."

After the Shema came the *Tefillah* or prayer. The ruler of the synagogue could call on any adult male of the congregation to perform this duty. The person praying usually stood before the chest of the rolls of Scriptures. The oldest form of the Tefillah consisted of a series of ascriptions or petitions, each of which ended in the benedictory response: "Blessed art thou, O Lord." About the close of the first century an

The Torah Ark at the Western Wall in Jerusalem.

Berthold Werner/Wikimedia Commons

arrangement was made in which there were eighteen of these prayers, from which the name "The Eighteen" (*Shemoneh Esreh*) was derived, a name that was maintained even when a nineteenth prayer was added. Prayers 1–3 were in praise of God; 4–16 were petitions; and 17–19 were thanksgivings. On Sabbaths and festival days only the first three and last three were recited.

The Scripture lesson that followed the Tefillah could be read by any member of the congregation, even children. The only exception was that at the Feast of Purim a minor was not allowed to read the book of Esther. If priests or Levites were present in the worship service, they were given precedence. The readers usually stood while reading (cf. Lk. 4:16).

Prescribed lessons out of the Pentateuch for special Sabbaths were established early. For other Sabbaths the reader himself chose the passage, but subsequently all the Pentateuchal readings became fixed. Sections, called *sedarim*, were established in order to complete the reading of the Pentateuch within a prescribed time. Babylonian Jews divided the Pentateuch into 154 sections and thus completed reading it in three years, whereas Palestinian Jews read it through once every year.

A lesson from the Prophets immediately followed the reading from the Pentateuch, a custom practiced already in NT times. When Jesus came to his hometown of Nazareth and entered the synagogue, he stood up to read, and the book of the prophet Isaiah was given to him (Lk. 4:16–17). It is not clear from this account whether or not Jesus himself chose the portion. He may have, because the readings from the Prophets were not fixed, and either the ruler of the synagogue or the reader could choose them. The prophetical lessons were usually considerably shorter than those from the Pentateuch. Translations often accompanied both readings. In Palestine the Scriptures were read in Hebrew, accompanied by an extemporaneous and free translation in Aramaic.

The sermon followed the reading from the Prophets (cf. Acts 13:15, where it is called a "message of encouragement"). That this was an important part of the synagogue service is revealed by the many references to teaching in the synagogue in the NT (Matt. 4:23; Mk. 1:21; 6:2; Lk. 4:15; 6:6; 13:10; Jn. 6:59; 18:20). The preacher usually sat (Lk. 4:20), but the Acts account has Paul standing (Acts 13:16). No single individual was appointed to do the preaching. Any competent worshipper might be invited by the ruler to bring the sermon for the day (Lk. 4:16–17; Acts 13:15).

The importance of the "freedom of the synagogue," as this custom was called, to the propagation of the gospel can scarcely be overemphasized. Jesus constantly went into the synagogues to teach, and everywhere Paul went he searched out the synagogue. The apostle took advantage of this custom not only that he might preach the Good News to his fellow countrymen but also so that he might reach the God-fearers. These were Gentiles who had become disillusioned with the old pagan religions and were attracted to Judaism because of its high ethical morality and its monotheistic faith. God-fearers had some familiarity with the Scriptures and proved to be ready recipients of the gospel.

Scribes and Rabbis

As noted earlier (see chap. 5), the term *scribe* is used to translate the Hebrew word *sopher* (plural *sopherim*). In the ancient world, relatively few people received the training necessary to gain skill in the art of writing, and

Scribe producing a Hebrew manuscript.

Kim Guess/www.BiblePlaces.com

those who followed the scribal profession were usually regarded as scholars (cf. the NIV translation of 1 Cor. 1:20) and could hold high civic offices. Especially after the Babylonian exile, Jewish scribes were involved not only in clerical activities, such as the copying of biblical manuscripts, but also in religious instruction. Accordingly, the NIV sometimes uses the rendering "teacher" in the OT (e.g., Ezra 7:6), and in the NT it consistently uses "teacher of the law."

In ancient Israel the scribal craft was principally confined to certain clans who doubtless preserved the trade as a family guild profession, passing the knowledge of this essential skill from father to son (cf. the "clans of scribes" dwelling at Jabez, 1 Chr. 2:55). During the monarchy a substantial number of scribes came from the Levites. The point of contact between the ritual and scribal functions derives from the demand for fiscal organization of temple operations (e.g., in Mesopotamia and Egypt most of the earliest writings are associated with temple records). A Levite recorded the priestly assignments (1 Chr. 24:6), and the royal scribe helped in counting the public funds collected for the repair of the temple (2 Ki. 12:10–11; 2 Chr. 14:11). Since the furnishing of written copies of the law was a (scribal) Levitical responsibility (Deut. 17:18), the reforms of Jehoshaphat (cf. 2 Chr. 17) cannot be disassociated from the scribal function.

Ezra marked the watershed for the later development of the understanding of the term *scribe*. The term is used in an administrative sense in Artaxerxes' royal decree (Ezra 7:12–26), but in the narrative (7:6, 11) the term already refers to Ezra as a scribe who, by reason of his learning, is capable of interpreting the law for the common people. Moreover, by his priestly lineage (7:6) he symbolized the close connection between the priesthood and this official interpretation of the law. This connection, which existed probably until the second century BC, appears to be the continuation of the association between scribal and cultic functions of an earlier day. By Persian royal decree, the law of Moses was made binding on Jews living west of the Euphrates River (7:25). The essential task of interpreting Moses' law so that it could function in this new civil capacity was given to the priesthood (Ezra) and the Levites (cf. Neh. 8:6–9).

During the next several centuries the priests exercised authority over the correct legal interpretation of the law, and the growing body of such interpretation came to be known as the *oral law*. It is clear, however, that the scribes played a major role in the development of this tradition. The rules and practices established by the scribes gradually acquired a binding authority within some Jewish groups; and eventually, after AD 70, their teaching became the basis of mainstream Judaism.

Already in the second century BC, the author of the Wisdom of Jesus ben Sirach (also known as Ecclesiasticus), spoke in praise of the "perfect scribe" (Sir. 38:24–39:11). This ode confirms the picture of a scribe as one schooled in the law and religious wisdom, understanding the implications of both the written law and oral traditions. As a result of his learning, he enjoyed a prominence in public assemblies and both understood and exercised justice among the people. Moreover, he was considered particularly pious by virtue of his knowledge of the revealed will of God, a feature of rabbinic understanding of piety.

In the Gospels, scribes are found in connection with both the Sadducees, a political-religious party that was priestly in character (e.g., Matt. 2:4; 21:15), and the Pharisees (cf. Matt. 23). The scholars of this latter group were the leaders of what was to become rabbinic Judaism; they came to be known as sages and as rabbis. But the scribes (scholars) of both parties challenged Jesus principally on his disobedience to traditional practice under the law (e.g., Mk. 2:16; 7:5).